They that Wait on the Lord

Neal Carlin

They that Wait on the Lord

An Uncharted Journey

the columba press

First published in 2014 by
the columba press
55A Spruce Avenue,
Stillorgan Industrial Park,
Blackrock, Co. Dublin

Cover design by redrattledesign.com
Origination by The Columba Press
Printed by ScandBook AB
All photographs © Neal Carlin

ISBN 978 1 78218 181 1

Cover and emblems

Depicted on the cover of this book is a sailing boat on a rough sea. My own journey, described in this book, and the journey of the Columba Community has undoubtedly been guided by the Holy Spirit. Nonetheless, it has been a challenging voyage in uncharted and, at times, stormy waters.

The cross acts as a compass for the journey. The cross, and all it stands for, is what we are called to go to and through, if the mystery of life, with its suffering and joy, is to yield the peace and consolation God wants for all of us.

May His good Spirit lead you in ways that are level and smooth. If choppy seas appear on your journey, like the storm that challenged the Apostles on the Sea of Galilee, know that Jesus is ever near. Both the wind and the sea obey Him. He will bring calm again.

Contents

Acknowledgements

I dedicate this book to all members of the Columba Community, past and present. We have journeyed together for the past thirty-five years and, with our faults and virtues, have helped form and, hopefully, reform each other on the way.

Thanks to Mary O'Donnell for encouragement, typing and re-typing this manuscript, and to Marguerite Hamilton and Tommy McCay, who both proofread and helped modify my utterances!

Many years ago my friend, Eugene Boyle, initiated the idea of this book. Then I got diverted, or delayed, with other ministries until the time was right.

Thanks also to Archbishop Eamon Martin, Armagh, in honouring me with his foreword and encouragement.

Richard Rohr, who has honoured me with his complimentary words on the cover of this book, has always been an inspirational figure in my life since the late seventies.

Neal Carlin,
May 2014,
www.columbacommunity.com

Foreword

At the launch of the Year of Faith in 2012, Pope Benedict XVI used a striking and beautiful image to describe our pilgrimage through life. Quoting Acts of the Apostles, he said: 'The door of faith is always open for us.' At the moment of our baptism we enter through that door and we set out on a journey that lasts a lifetime. Indeed, the journey continues beyond death and on into eternal life.

In recent years many parishes, in their missions, retreats and novenas, have allowed the opportunity for committed lay women and men to share their 'faith story', to deliver their personal 'testimony of faith'. These inspiring reflections affirm the way that God works in and through the lives of all of us, calling us over and over again to conversion and a deepening of our friendship with Him, inviting us again and again to cross the threshold of faith and set out on the new adventures that He has in mind for us. A friend of mine often reminds me of that old quip: 'If you want to make God laugh – tell Him your plans!' And it's true that usually what we have in mind for our own faith journey is not what God has in store for us. The challenge is to generously open ourselves up to God's plan and allow God to lead us.

In *They that Wait on the Lord*, Fr Neal Carlin offers us his testimony, his 'faith story', a personal and honest reflection on his fifty years of priesthood. I often meditate on the phrase 'led by the Spirit' which occurs several times in Acts of the Apostles. Peter is 'led by the Spirit' to the house of Cornelius; Philip is 'led by the Spirit' to converse with, and convert the Ethiopian eunuch; Paul and his companions are 'led by the Spirit' on the great missionary journeys. For me, the phrase encapsulates the sense that the mission of the Church is in God's hands, not ours. If we think that we can sit down and plan great strategies to save the world according to our own designs, then we shouldn't be surprised if we find God laughing! The Holy Spirit guides the Church's mission; our challenge is to open ourselves up to the Spirit's promptings and allow the Spirit to 'melt us, mould us, fill us and use us' as God wills.

Fr Neal shares how he was 'led by the Spirit' throughout his life. Very early in his ministry, he became aware of the importance of 'waiting upon the Lord', and realised, as he says himself, that 'God's hand is above all the hands that attempt to control our lives' – even our own! His powerful testimony helps us to realise that, even in our darkest moments, God provides; the Spirit can quietly make things happen. Reflecting back on things with the benefit of hindsight, we discover, as the well-known saying puts it, that God has been writing straight, even with crooked lines.

I wish that more priests would share with us, as Fr Neal does here, their stories of faith. I believe that many priests have powerful testimonies to give about how God worked through them during dark times of conflict and struggle for the Church and the community. At this time in Ireland, it would be enriching and perhaps even cathartic if more priests were inspired to offer their testimony of a life lived in service of God and the People of God. In the fifty years or so since the Second Vatican Council, so much has shifted and changed in the familiar surroundings of priests and people in the Church. To some extent it might be said that we have 'lost our bearings'. The awful and shocking child abuse scandals, the decline in vocations and the rapid secularisation of Ireland have sapped our morale. The terrible violence and conflict in Ireland have ripped our community apart and left deep wounds and scars that are still in need of healing. But through it all, many committed priests and lay people opened themselves up to God's plan for them, allowing themselves to be led by the Spirit. In this way they have brought God's compassion, healing, solace and comfort to so many people and at the same time have written new adventures and chapters in their personal stories of faith and ministry.

Looking back on his life journey, Fr Neal is able to discern the workings of the Spirit, opening new doors and possibilities for him down through the years. Certainly the fruits of the Spirit in his ministry are rich – the Columba community and YARD (Young Adults' Reality Dreams) project; the St Anthony's Retreat Centre and Hermitages; the White Oaks Rehabilitation Centre and Acorn Project; the Celtic Prayer Garden and IOSAS Centre. Although these may be the tangible and more obvious 'outcomes' of his ministry, we all know that Fr Neal's deep spiritual presence and witness have borne countless other hidden fruits and touched and healed the lives of many marginalised people.

The door of faith is always open for us and God is constantly calling us to have the courage to cross that threshold and be prepared for anything! I hope and pray that many will read Fr Neal's testimony and be stirred to believe that anything is possible, if only they can allow themselves to be led by the Spirit.

+Eamon Martin

9 June 2014

Introduction

Nestled at the foot of the Lammermuir Hills on the southern edge of East Lothian, in Scotland, Santa Maria Abbey was the Cistercian sanctuary sought out by Derry-born, Fr Neal Carlin when he found himself at a crossroads in his life in late autumn 1978.

Sitting alone in his room on a cold November evening, following his arrival at the Nunraw monastery for a retreat to discern God's will for him, the thirty-eight-year-old had felt tired to the point of exhaustion.

His traumatic departure from St Eugene's in Derry City, back home in Ireland, had left him feeling disillusioned. However, amid the feelings of hurt, disappointment, and questioning of the diocesan system of church governance, he also had a sense of calm, especially when he prayed.

Deep down inside, he had a quiet confidence that good would come from this; that this was the beginning of a new freedom, and a new apostolate.

This feeling was strengthened after the third day of his stay in the monastery, when during prayer he received an image of a slow flying eagle using its powerful wings to get off the ground, along with the word 'wait'.

This is one of many spiritual experiences shared by Fr Neal in the pages of this book, as he reflects on an eventful journey travelled in faith, that took him to America and Mexico to experience emerging new communities and houses of prayer, and led to the foundation of the Columba Community in his home city in the midst of the Troubles.

Just like the saying, from little acorns great oaks grow, the Columba Community, in glorifying God, has grown in its ministry of prayer, healing, reconciliation and building community, to provide a house of prayer and reconciliation, a centre of retreat, a rehabilitation centre for those suffering from alcohol, drug and gambling addictions, a Celtic prayer garden and visitor centre commemorating the Irish saints, and a conference centre and residential campus, known as 'The Sanctuary', to encourage interaction between communities and groups from different religious and tribal backgrounds.

In a further example of what happens following listening prayer by a believing community, the Columba Community also launched the YARD (Young Adults' Reality Dreams) project two years before its thirtieth anniversary.

As the story of the Columba Community unfolds, the reader gets an insight into the person of Fr Neal Carlin, from the formation of his faith in childhood to his ordination to the priesthood, and his ever developing openness thereafter to being led by the Holy Spirit.

Some reflections written by Fr Neal over the years have been included in the book, and give us an insight into his love of nature and the Celtic soul, which sees God in all things. He seems to see the sacred and the hand of God in the ordinary.

Celebrating fifty years in the priesthood, Fr Neal also shares his vision for the Church of the future and his hope that small basic communities, like the Columba Community, will 'sprout up all over Ireland, like small springs to again irrigate this holy land of ancient saints and scholars'.

Mary O'Donnell

Kairos

When the Columba Community of Prayer and Reconciliation celebrated its thirtieth anniversary, the community members agreed that it was a Kairos – an opportune time – for revealing the full story of the origins of the community and how God has blessed us and our apostolate.

After a seventeen-year wait, the Columba Community received Canonical Acceptance into the Derry Diocese in 1995, when Bishop Seamus Hegarty gave the official recognition during a special ceremony at Mass in St Eugene's Cathedral, which was attended by over one thousand people. Many of those present had benefited over the years from our community's healing ministry and its good counsel during the years of trouble in the north of Ireland.

This book tells the story of our small, basic Christian community. It is a story of what God will do with a group of people who pray, listen and obey.

The Columba Community of Prayer and Reconciliation is a small dedicated group of Christians, formed in Derry and on the Donegal border during thirty years of the Troubles, who have worked consistently for peace and reconciliation.

Our story is one of 'waiting on the Lord' (Isaiah 40:31) and of serving the marginalised. It is a story of a faith-walk that has had extraordinary results in healing people, and in forming God's Kingdom on earth.

Having opened five pastoral care centres, with thirty-five full-time employees, and many more volunteers, we want to promote this model of building the Kingdom of God. The hope is that this model will be imitated by praying groups and Christian leaders throughout Ireland, and beyond.

It is interesting to note that Pope Francis gave his wholehearted endorsement to the basic Christian community movements who met recently from all over Brazil. Here, Pope Francis talked of basic communities' 'most important role in the Church's evangelising mission', and quoted his *Evangelii Gaudium*: 'Base communities bring to the Church a new enthusiasm for evangelisation and a capacity for dialogue with the world that renew the Church', provided that they maintain links with the parish and the diocese.

Any Church that is serious about reform, renewal and evangel-isation, as well as forming appropriate governance systems, would do well to study the background, ethos, and achievements of the Columba Community of Prayer and Reconciliation.

For the model and formation of our community, we point to the Celtic Church and, especially, Colmcille/Columba the Reconciler. The other source of inspiration is the movement of the Holy Spirit in the Acts of the Apostles and in the church of the diaspora.

Diaspora seems a most appropriate word, considering my personal story. Originally ordained for the Diocese of Motherwell, in Scotland, I worked happily there in parishes and secondary schools, with youth clubs and athletic clubs, for eleven years. Then, in 1975, I returned to my native Diocese of Derry, with the agreement of being incardinated there after an initial period of two years. However, in late October 1978, when more than three years had passed, I was suddenly recalled to Scotland. No reason was given.

What happened after that is told in the following story of my faith journey, which highlights the need to pray in times of crisis and ask, 'What is God's will?', and to remember that His hand is above all the hands that shape our lives. As we read in Genesis

45:8, Joseph said to his brothers 'So it was not you who sent me here but God.'

God's hand and His will are what matters. It is not what happens to us in life so much as how we see it, and how we react. Our sense of autonomy and maturity as Christians, and indeed our general well-being, seem to depend largely on how we are guided, or behave, in times of adversity.

Being guided by the Holy Spirit's gifts is what has given the Columba Community a Pentecostal flavour. This quality is essential if the Irish Catholic Church is ever to become a light to the nation, as it was in the distant past.

*The lessons of life
are from the journey taken,
not the destination.*

The Call 'to Wait'

My story begins at what was a major turning point in my life as a priest. In 1964 I was ordained in St Peter's, Wexford, for the Diocese of Motherwell. My decision to begin my priestly ministry in Scotland had been largely influenced by friends who had gone there ahead of me, and I worked happily in the diocese, both in parish work and schools, until 1975.

Around that time, the Troubles were raging in Northern Ireland. I had always been interested in the work of reconciliation between Protestants and Catholics in Ireland, and requested a transfer to work in the Derry Diocese.

After agreement by both Bishop Frank Thomson, of Motherwell, and Bishop Edward Daly, of Derry, I was appointed as a curate to St Eugene's Cathedral, in my home city, in 1975.

I was enjoying working in the parish as well as in St Joseph's Secondary School, and leading the large St Joseph's charismatic prayer group I had founded. But in late autumn 1978, after three years and three months at St Eugene's, everything suddenly changed.

I received a letter from Bishop Thomson saying that Bishop Daly had asked that I be recalled to Scotland. To my knowledge, no reason was ever given for this, which annoyed not only me but also Bishop Thomson, who welcomed me back to Scotland.

Disappointed, disillusioned and alone on leaving St Eugene's, and needing time and peace to pray and discern the future, I got permission from Bishop Thomson to go on a four-day retreat to the remote Cistercian Abbey in Nunraw, Scotland. From previous visits, I knew it to be a place of great prayer and contemplation.

In the early morning of the third day of my retreat, I was trying to pray. I felt tired and vulnerable as I read my breviary. I think I was burned-out and was praying on my own power, and so did not feel led by God's Spirit.

As well as fulfilling the duties of a priest working in a busy parish, my involvement with the charismatic group back in Derry had resulted in more people coming to me for confession in the cathedral, and many asking me to pray with them, give counsel and spiritual direction.

This left me with little time for private prayer, and so some burnout was probably inevitable. It was only following the shock of being asked to leave the cathedral, and some resultant sleepless nights, that I came to realise just how tired I actually was.

With hindsight, I would now question the use of charismatic gifts by a priest governed by institutional rules and the requirements that go with working in such a large parish. While it may work for some, undoubtedly there is tension.

My faith came alive by attending prayer meetings and through the use of the gifts of the Spirit, but there was a tension between the requirements of institutional rules and the use of the gifts of the Spirit encouraged in the charismatic movement, which to me are the tools for building Christ's Church.

I will say more about this later as I believe it augurs well for a new system of governance, that is, a basic Christian community setting where one is accompanied in his/her prayers for protection and discernment.

Unless we have that, we can suffer from oppression resulting from ministering on one's own. After all, it is a spiritual battle and we need time out, the support of companions, and the discernment that comes from our brothers and sisters who are praying. From my vantage point now, it seems to me that unity of vision, at least, is needed between the parish priest and the curate if charismatic gifts are to be used within the ministry of the parish.

On the third day of my retreat at Nunraw Abbey, I got an image in my mind as I prayed of an eagle flying slowly as I prayed. It was really pushing its wings to keep itself up. At the same time, I got this sense 'to wait', and I felt that I was being told not to work on my own power, but to wait on a higher power.

I had a real hope of something new, and recalled a dream I'd had about a month earlier. On reflection, that dream had somewhat prepared me for the disappointment of being moved from the cathedral parish.

I had dreamed that I was walking along the seashore and put one foot in the water. In the dream, I then woke up from a sleep to find myself floating out at sea, with no land in sight. I was perfectly at ease. I could see a fishing net nearby and thought, perhaps a fishing boat will return for it later and pick me up. I then fell back to sleep, perfectly relaxed, in a floating position.

As I have a healthy respect and even fear of the sea, I was aware on waking that this was a special and significant dream. Having done some work on dreams since, I now accept the meaning of this one for my life.

As I see it, the dream was preparing me for my time adrift, and being comparatively free from the diocesan system. I felt I was being told to step out in faith and not to be afraid in this new situation. It was about trusting in God's timing and His ways.

Looking back at over thirty years as a secular priest with a unique calling, I have, above all, a great sense of awe and gratitude to God for His ways.

Following the sense 'to wait', I felt the need to ask my bishop for permission for six months' sabbatical to visit some of the basic Christian communities emerging in the United States and South America at that time, as a result of the spiritual revival spearheaded by the charismatic movement of the late sixties and seventies.

Bishop Thomson had already welcomed me back to Scotland, and had spoken about me resuming work as a curate to a good friend of mine, Fr Joe Martin, from Co. Donegal. However, he granted me the sabbatical and, with a letter of recommendation, I set off to spend the first six months of 1979 in America.

A priest friend arranged for me to stay in a students' hostel in St Monica's Parish, Los Angeles, and on a table in my room there was a piece of wood with an inscription carved on it that riveted my attention. It read: 'Young men may grow weary and faint but they that wait upon the Lord shall renew their strength. They shall mount up with wings as eagles; they will run and not grow weary, walk and not grow weak.' It was a quote from Isaiah 40:31.

After receiving the image of a large eagle in flight while I was at Nunraw Abbey, with a strong sense that I was to wait, I had asked a good friend of mine, who knew the Bible well, if there was anything in it about 'waiting' and 'an eagle'. He could not find anything and yet here was the inclusive text!

I remember taking the piece of wood out into the corridor and telling the first people I met how I had come six thousand miles to get this text. They must have thought I was crazy. I was excited and more convinced than ever about the need to wait on the Lord.

About two months later, I was at a large prayer meeting in El Paso attended by about eight hundred people. During the meeting, the leader, who was a young priest called Fr Joe Nolan, stood up and said: 'I have had a Scripture given to me three times this week and I know it is for someone here.'

Instinctively, I knew that Isaiah 40:31 was the Scripture he was going to read. And he did! He kept repeating it, but I did not have the courage to say out in front of everyone that it was for me. Afterwards, I went up to him and he prayed with me.

Sometime later, I was in Hope House, Newark, New Jersey, and was relating this story to a Fr Bob Brennan as we stood in the corridor outside his room. Smiling, he opened his door and pointed to a wall which had a poster with a beautiful picture of an eagle drawn on it and the words of Isaiah 40:31. He gave it to me to take home.

Perhaps, the most powerful of these revelations on the call to wait and trust was when I returned to Ireland and negotiated with Bishop Thomson to have my sabbatical extended.

I had an appointment in Armagh with Cardinal Tomas O'Fiaich, who had spoken to Bishop Thomson during a meeting in Rome about me working with prisoners across the divide.

I was on my way for lunch with the cardinal, after having celebrated two Masses in the notorious Long Kesh prison, when I realised that I was early. Feeling thirsty, I left the motorway to call into Craigavon for a cup of tea. As I approached a roundabout, I was literally praying for direction and felt that I should go right. As I turned right, I saw a man walking a dog and stopped to ask him where I could get a cup of tea.

He smiled, told me that there would not be any place open, and insisted that I come to his house. So we got the dog into the back of the car, and off we went. I remember he was called Dickie, and he told me that he had once played football for the Republic of Ireland.

As we drove alongside kerbs painted red, white and blue, Dickie mentioned that it was 'a loyalist housing estate'. I told him that it was an ecumenical day for me as I had been with the Provos in Long Kesh prison that morning.

In we went to his house and, while he was in the kitchen making tea, I reached for a book of Bible quotations which was sitting on the table. Opening it near the middle, I again saw in black print the Scripture, Isaiah 40:31, 'they that wait upon the

Lord …'. I remember asking the Lord what this all meant. And the answer came, clear as a bell: 'You are going to see Cardinal O'Fiaich. He is a good man, but I told you to wait on me.'

I went on to meet the Cardinal, but I knew that whatever he offered me I was to wait upon the Lord. So, when he asked me if I would like to come to Armagh and work in the prison or a parish, or both, I hesitated. He then asked if I would like time to think about it and I said that I would.

I wrote to him a few days later, relating my experience of receiving the Scripture of Isaiah 40:31 four times in Scotland and America, and then just before I went to visit him, and I told him that I very much appreciated the offer, but felt I was meant to wait on the Lord and trust His guidance.

The Cardinal wrote back a lovely letter of appreciation, encouraging me to continue to wait on the Lord's guidance and enclosing a donation towards my work. He seemed to respect the fact that the Spirit was guiding me.

So, for me, this was the beginning of a listening time, during which I reflected on my experience of the new emerging Christian communities I had visited in the United States, and especially the work for the poor at Juarez, in Mexico.

The Pecos Community in New Mexico was, perhaps, the most influential of the new emerging Christian communities that I visited. This was a development by a Benedictine monastery of a lay community comprised generally of students who had just finished college and had yet to start work, or even choose a career.

They would come for a year or two and, subsequently, some of them became novices and others postulants, and joined the Benedictines. The majority spent one year learning about inner healing, forgiveness, and how to develop their charismatic gifts.

The profound and enthusiastic teaching of Christian truths there left a deep impression on me. I came away with a newfound respect for mixed community, and the aid towards emotional and spiritual development that such an environment provides.

The discipline and mutual affection that is born of a deep trust in Jesus, and in one another, certainly challenged the more stifling rules some of us were given in seminary days.

Apart from the Benedictines, other religious men and women spent some years with the Pecos Community, either giving directed retreats or moving out from that base to give parish retreats or lectures.

A nun called Sister Marian helped me with a private retreat. We reflected together on my childhood, growing up in a family of ten, and the choice of priesthood. Among other exercises she gave me, one in particular stands out. She sensed that I had some deep faith in Jesus as Saviour and Lord, and asked me to climb the nearby mountain one afternoon and let God the Father show me the beauty of creation.

It was a barren desert mountain and, coming from the hills of Donegal where I always had a beautiful view of the sea, I struggled to see much beauty there in New Mexico. I looked at every dried up twig and questioned what on earth I was doing up there.

But something important happened on that desert mountain. I got in touch with my childhood, with the sense of security that the Heavenly Father brings, and I asked Jesus to give me His relationship with His Father and our Father, and to heal my relationship with my earthly father.

I recalled my early childhood and the songs we used to listen to, my father and mother singing together, and the good fun we had as a family – hunting, fishing, football and films.

I also recalled some of the pain that happened when my father drank too much or got angry. I had the sense that one or two other members of the family had suffered more from this and I felt sad. It was the first time I had got in touch with some causes of insecurity and difficulty in our lives as individuals in a close-knit family.

However, there were also attributes my father had which my brothers, sisters and I have been blessed by. Indeed, his sense of justice and his sense of humour have had a big influence on all our lives.

I sensed a degree of peace, compassion and comfort on that mountain, and began to relax in believing that the Father, who loves us all with an infinite love, would bring healing, energy and vision into my life again.

I recall a special time I had with my father on returning from the United States. My spiritual director in Pecos had suggested that I tell my father I loved him. So one night, as we watched the television fade and go off the air, we started talking. I got around to saying: 'My spiritual director said that I should tell you that I love you.' At this, my father got off his chair and we shook hands, and as we parted he said: 'We Irishmen find these things difficult to say, don't we? Thanks and good night.'

It was during those six weeks in Pecos, New Mexico, that the vision of building basic Christian communities made sense to me. I looked at my own character and needs, apart from the call to serve other people, and I sensed that the need for company and supportive human relationships was very important.

Through my experience with the charismatic prayer group in Derry, and the knowledge of small communities growing up throughout the world, I yearned for a small, basic Christian community.

Reflecting back on it, I realise now that God had heard that cry from the depth of my soul and indirectly facilitated that to happen. I suppose that is what gave me a sense of peace amid the feelings of hurt I experienced on being recalled from the Derry Diocese. What happened was God's way of bringing about what I desired, and it has been a great blessing.

This call 'to wait' is an ongoing call to all of us who call ourselves Christian. For me, the waiting, in one sense, culminated in getting Columba House in the spring of 1980.

In another sense, the waiting on the Lord, and being guided by His will, is the story of the listening prayer and the story of the other centres founded over the last thirty years by the Columba Community of Prayer and Reconciliation.

It is an ongoing call to a way of life. It is a call to discern daily how to listen, to pray, and to work. It is to wait and pay attention to the Spirit of Jesus, who desires to live in each of us, to obey the Father, to pray in us and, with His gifts, to build up His people and teach them how to live in His Kingdom.

On this theme of listening, I recall the joy and excitement experienced when I went to the cinema to see *Chariots of Fire* in the mid-eighties. It is the story of a modest, but exceptionally talented athlete called Eric Liddell, who ran in the 1924 Olympics in Paris. He was aiming to run the one hundred metres when he learned that the heats were to be run on a Sunday. As a strict Christian from the north of Scotland, whose missionary parents would have regarded such activity as breaking the Sabbath, he refused to take part in the race. Instead, he switched with another British athlete called Harold Abrahams. Liddell ran in the four hundred metres competition and won a gold medal.

As I watched the film, I witnessed an amazing thing. On the Sunday, Liddell went to church in Paris and was depicted as reading a piece of Scripture and preaching on it. The Scripture he read was Isaiah 40:31, 'They that wait upon the Lord shall renew their strength. They shall mount up with wings as eagles; they will run and not grow weary, walk and not grow weak.'

He paraphrased this text to make the point that those who trust the Lord will not be disappointed, and that those who honour the Lord will be honoured by the Lord. The next day, a member of the American Olympic squad slipped Liddell a note which read, 'The Lord honours those who honour him.'

This, to my mind, underpins the Christian philosophy of life that has been the basis for our development in the Columba Community. This glorifies God and brings blessing to his people, which is the purpose of this book.

The words 'to wait on the Lord and His will' are central to all our lives, and important for each Christian each day. And it has been an ongoing theme for our community as we meet to reflect on life and possible new works.

The Cost of Discipleship

Yesterday he felt the strong wind of the wild ocean on his face.
Yet he travelled the course he sensed was laid out for him.
It took him beyond the chartered waters
of the conventional journey,
on a way that offered pain, gain, excitement and challenge.
It demanded vigour and strength of youth renewed.
There is the sense of ever-new lands to be discovered.
There are new adventures and new challenges.
We meet new people who speak or write and remind us
how good and filled with compassion God really is.
But the cost is real, when we step out in obedience to the still,
small voice within.

So let us not minimise the pain and the sense of excommunication
and the times past when loneliness has struck.
To be misrepresented or dealt with unjustly by another,
or by the institution one has trusted,
is a reality for some on their path to freedom.
Yet all things, Paul says, 'work together unto good
for those that trust the Lord'.
The Way will surely bring self-doubt that only disperses in prayer,
for this is a spiritual journey and
God alone sustains the soul on the Way.
We are required then to listen, to read His word.
We are sent angels on the way.

Jim Burke was one of those.
He always encouraged me
and the Columba Community to stay free,
to wait, and to develop and serve as led by the Spirit.

This Way, understood and followed by some fellow travellers,
was the way to Life, the way to Truth,
the way to true Freedom.
It gave the reason for living.
This was simply The Way.
The ways of the Lord are bigger than any Church way,
bigger than any one religious way.
We find Him in our weakness.
We see him in the wounded self and in the wounds of others.
It is there we find Him in his entire Peace and Presence.
May you find Him today.
Let Him, as the Loving Father of the prodigal son, find you.
He is always on the lookout for you.

If prayer is a raising up of mind and heart to God,
then Lord, come and raise up my mind to where I can visualise
what is best.
Raise up my heart so that your courage in me
will allow me to move towards what is best.
I need confidence to cast out fear.
I need to trust your call to Greatness, your call to Transcendence.
Without a vision, your people perish and nobody, especially You,
wants that.

The Holy Mountain

These days, the mountain glows with pink and purple heather.
The bright green grass is interspersed with small bushes
and granite rocks gleaming in the morning sun.
Like a blushing bride full of conscious beauty,
the mountain, at this time of year, comes into full bloom.
She seems to speak loud and clear
for those who have ears to hear and eyes to see.
She seems to say: 'Life is worthwhile.'
She recalls the past, when thirty years ago, exactly,
the torrential rain filled the small enclave,
holding water near the top of the mountain.
The high lake overflowed, then broke its banks
and caused a landslide.
Large sods of heather and soil were swept down the hillside
by the ever increasing torrent of gushing tons of water.
The residents in one house fled for safety
as the rocks, mud and earth slid past their door.
Then, the calm came again.
For some time the hillside,
like a soldier after the war,
showed its ugly open wounds.
It took time to heal.
Today, however, what once looked ugly and disfigured
has now turned into something attractive.
As someone once said,

'Our illnesses and wounds do not diminish our beauty.
They define our beauty.'
The once ugly gorge
has now turned into a valley of green grass and small bushes,
a place where sheep graze and seem to love to be,
a place where birds now sing and nest.
This area provides shelter from the wind.
What once seemed like a disaster has turned to good.
This is the way of nature.
This is the way of God.
We should never be afraid or run away.

Childhood Memories

Born on 1 May 1940 in the Waterside area of Derry, in a large farmhouse in the country known as Ballyowen House, I was the third child in a family of ten – seven boys and three girls – born to Neal and May Carlin.

During the writing of this book, I paid a visit to my old home up on the hill overlooking Gransha Hospital. The house has been empty for about twenty years now, but is still standing intact with a good slate roof.

I stood there on the cobblestone street imagining what it was like, and recalled the stories my parents told us about times past. One was a sad story of how my grandfather had fallen on that street one winter's night, after putting away the pony and trap. He'd had too much to drink and lay there too long. He got pneumonia and died shortly afterwards. In those days, they did not have the medicine we have now to treat such patients. My father was just six years of age then. The death had a profound effect on him and he spoke of it occasionally.

My father owned a business that had been founded by his grandfather, also Neal Carlin, around 1860. It began as a grocery shop, then a pub in Cross Street and later a wholesale wine and spirits business, which also opened onto Clooney Terrace, in Derry.

The present Carlin Terrace in the Waterside is named after my great grandfather, a developer of the original Carlin Street. A copy of his will shows that he left eighteen houses to his daughter, my grand-aunt Cassie. He certainly was a developer.

He began his first grocery shop by selling salt in small bags at the doorsteps of the city's homes. From there, he developed a reputable wholesale Wine and Spirit Merchants, and bottled 'Neal Carlin' Guinness. In those days, the Guinness consumer in Derry could tell the difference in taste of the Guinness depending on how it was stored and who bottled it, even before reading the label on the bottle.

In the early 1940s, during the war years, we left Ballyowen House and moved into the city and then over the border to Donegal, partly to escape from the constant harassing visits to our house by the Royal Ulster Constabulary (RUC). My father was known for his nationalist views and for being the sponsor of the 'Neal Carlin Cup' for Gaelic football in north Co. Derry, and so found himself the target of attention from the police.

My mother often talked of the RUC banging on the door at two or three o'clock in the morning, 'checking up on Republicans'. She would have to get up and make them tea, for if she did not they would return two or three times in a week. Back then, there was no redress, and nobody in authority to appeal to for justice.

It was frustrating and demeaning for my father, and others subjected to similar treatment. Such behaviour formed part of the build-up to what was to erupt many years later in the violent rebellion following the civil rights campaign of the late sixties. Thanks be to God, and to those who worked hard and suffered for civil rights, things seem better today.

At that time there were four of us, two boys and two girls. After living for a couple of years in Derry, we moved eleven miles to Newtowncunningham, in Co. Donegal. The rural setting gave us plenty of freedom. With fishing and hunting opportunities, my brother and I look back on happy times, amid hard times as well.

We, as a family, on the one hand were known locally to have property in Derry, yet we also experienced a degree of poverty like most of our schoolmates in the mid-forties and early fifties.

The local large farmers were Protestants, so when we studied history, and the Plantation of Ulster in particular, we had already become familiar with the results.

The good arable land in that Lagan Valley, of east Donegal, was given to Scottish farmers by the British during 'the plantation' that followed the flight of the Earls from Rathmullan, in the early sixteen hundreds.

Back then, we were given two weeks off school annually in October so that we could gather potatoes, or 'spuds' as we called them, for the local farmers. Yet, it must be said, there was mutual respect between the traditional Irish and what became known as the Scots Irish sections of the community. In fact, I recall members of the Hibernian pipe band and the local Orange band swapping musical instruments with each other for their parade days on the twelfth of July and the fifteenth of August.

Indeed, there were pranks played also. My father, for example, was known to have swapped the flags so that, on the morning of the twelfth of July, the Tricolour flew from the top of the Orange Hall instead of the Union Jack!

At an early age, I sensed that God was real and active in our lives. In later years, one of my sisters told me a story from our childhood. Word had reached our village in Donegal that someone, in some part of the world, had been told in prophesy the date that the world would end. Today, we would refer to it as Armageddon, the final reckoning.

When the moment arrived, that day back in 1950 or thereabouts, my brothers and sisters were found hiding under the kitchen table, and I was missing. I was later found up in the attic, kneeling in prayer at a small dressing table that had flowers on it. I was praying that all the family would meet in Heaven. It must have been October or May time, as we used to do up an altar in the attic in honour of Our Lady.

Apparently, I was that kind of child. However, it would not have been unexpected to have strong faith as the practice of praying together at six o'clock every evening, usually the Rosary, was very common in our village.

As children, my brother and I often got 'caught for the Rosary', as the saying went, in going to visit friends when they were about to pray. Another memory is of learning Latin when I was ten years old from my mother and the village schoolmaster, in order to be able to serve at Mass. This was a common experience for boys in the village.

However, it would be wrong to think that we were 'Holy Joes'. We 'progged' orchards with the rest of the boys. 'Progged' sounds better than 'stole', and seems, on reflection, to have been an acceptable behaviour for our age group in the autumn, in an area where some great apples and pears were grown.

It is strange how certain behaviour patterns become socially acceptable. I am sure that if we had damaged trees, or property, our conscience would not have excused us, nor would that have been socially acceptable.

In those days, on returning from a Sunday afternoon hunting rabbits or from the 'banking', where we played football, it was quite common to stave off the hunger by uprooting a small turnip, hitting it on a stone, or gate, and eating some of it. Today, that could be regarded as a healthy organic diet, or making sure you got your one in five.

We had little money to buy sweets. If we saved up money from gathering blackberries or 'spuds', we used some of that for the weekly visit to the 'pictures' and to buy a small bag of chips for four pence. Those were the highlights for a child aged ten or twelve years old in those days.

My brother Joe and I had an added exciting hobby that, for some reason, was not participated in by our peer group, and that was fishing brown trout down by the 'banking', the local name for a small river that ran eventually to Lough Swilly.

We still talk about those happy days. School could not end soon enough at a certain time of the year. We would often set the lines overnight and find fish in them the next day. Like the rabbits, fish formed part of our diet so we had an added incentive to develop hobbies of hunting.

My sister Angela and I set ten snares one late autumn in a stubble field. The next day, a Saturday, we went back to find that we had caught nine rabbits. That was the biggest catch we ever had in one day and, considering that we got five shillings a pair, we were well rewarded for our work.

On another windy night, instead of attending October Devotions in the local chapel, Joe and I went through the fields to examine our snares. Confident that we would have a catch on such a windy night, we gave into the temptation to take a flashlight and dodge the Church service. We did get a rabbit but were spotted by the other boys returning from Devotions, and they threatened to tell our parents. I think they were more jealous that we had caught the rabbit than they were worried about the state of our souls. Anyway, my mother would have just laughed and my father was not that 'Gospel greedy', so we felt happy with our night's work.

It occurs to me how simple life was and how little it took to amuse us. Joe and I still recall the Saturdays we spent walking up and down a field beside a local ploughman, as he neatly ploughed two drills at a time, with two horses that seemed to understand each other perfectly as they worked and turned in unison. It was either that or listen to Dick Barton on the radio on a Saturday morning, as television was unheard of locally at the time.

The experience of ploughing and harvesting left a lasting impression on my young mind. Even now, when I find myself writing about the land it leaves me feeling relaxed. There is something very soothing about memories of the trees, brooks and fields where we played. Now, when I hear my young nephews speak about hideouts and shelters they have built by the river, and on the mountains, those feelings for the land of my youth return.

My mum's faith

A short time before my mother died in 1999, she and I were having a conversation about the reality of God and when His presence was being experienced, as opposed to times in the past when He seemed far away. My mother said that she had always felt that God was very close, and I could see that. She came through a pretty tough life, yet retained an optimism and joy that came out in a very real way.

Her faith was not naïve or superstitious, like I have witnessed sometimes in women of her age. She possessed a belief in the essentials of Catholic teaching. Once, when we were discussing the possibility of 'limbo' many years ago, she said: 'I never for a minute believed that nonsense, even when it was common to do so. I never told the priest that, as I did not want to upset him if he did believe in limbo.' Now there is maturity.

She spoke out her prayers in a matter-of-fact way, and I remember one she uttered in her older years at Mass in St Anthony's, during a summer holiday when we had more than our share of rain. She prayed: 'God, please send some good weather and sunshine. The faces of the children are very pale.' A religious sister, who had lived at St Anthony's for some years as a hermit, reminded me of that in a letter following my mother's death.

Mum took to charismatic meetings very naturally, as she was greatly aware of the benefits to our communities of such prayer meetings and ministry. That sense of closeness to God is something that I certainly would have identified with as a child. In later years, after my Baptism in the Spirit experience, that sense of the reality of God's presence increased, or was it just that we began to express it more?

Whenever people ask me about my vocation to the priesthood, I recall going into the chapel to pray on the way home from school. In those days we prayed to Our Lady. I remember, as a twelve-year-old going on thirteen, offering a prayer to Our Lady that I would offer my life to the priesthood if I got through secondary school. They call it bargaining prayer. I really meant it, and this came back to me when I was about to do my leaving certificate.

Later, I was into football and athletics in a big way, going to dances and getting to enjoy the company of girls when I was seventeen or eighteen years old, yet the thoughts of priesthood persisted. I even shared it with a girl I was becoming close to. The way I looked at it was that I had made a commitment as a very young adolescent and, unless I was given some sign that I should not be a priest, I would become a priest. Yet, I could never visualise myself as a legalistic type of person, who would see things in black and white terms, and my family background would certainly not have conditioned me to lead a rigorous way of life, or lay emphasis on rules.

I remember taking part in a retreat in secondary school when I was about thirteen or fourteen years old. The retreat director's sermon was in keeping with the way things were in the early fifties. I got the sense from this priest that people who did not go to Mass were committing a mortal sin, and would be condemned to hell by God.

I spoke to him afterwards about my father not going to Sunday Mass regularly. I always had a difficulty condemning people who did not go to Mass and yet this priest was emphatic about how wrong it was. In my childhood, I could not see it that way. I loved and cared for my father, and could not condemn him for not going to Mass. This was prior to the advent of popular psychology that considered excusing causes and mitigating circumstances, which gave reasons for why some people behaved differently.

Our own life experiences colour how we interpret laws, regulations and commandments. A compassionate understanding of my father would have led me to believe that life was not always black and white, that there were also grey areas. This was especially so when I got older, and understood my father's own sense of loss.

He was six years old when his father died at thirty-three years of age. My grand-uncle, James, died when he was eighteen, and both he and my grandfather were quite heavy drinkers. I later found out that, as small children, their live-in Donegal nanny had been giving them whiskey in their hot milk. This acted as a quick sedative and made the nanny's job easier, but had repercussions later.

To understand one's own character and personality, it is important that we know something about our ancestry, especially our more recent ancestry. If we do not understand why we feel the way we do, the danger is that we become what we hate or have not accepted. It is known as the cycle of transmission of wounds or, to quote the eminent Swiss psychologist, Carl Jung, 'what we do not deal with in ourselves eventually deals with us'. We either transform our wounded state or we transmit it so that others also suffer.

School days
As our family increased my parents decided to search for a bigger home. I was thirteen when we moved to live in Fahan. Our new home, 'Kilmora' was, and still is, a family home, which is a joy to visit.

I went to secondary school earlier than most of my peers, and was the second youngest in the class. My brother Joe, a year-and-a-half older than me, was held back and I was pushed forward so that we could go to boarding school together.

We attended St Eunan's College, in Letterkenny, as boarders. It was an all-Irish college and all that was Gaelic was reinforced in me. I came from a soccer-playing area, and when I went to boarding school I got the strap around the legs a few times for breaking the rules and playing soccer. Thank God that narrow-minded rule has changed.

A group of us would play soccer during a short break between studies in the evenings, and I remember one time we were seen by the vice president of the college, who was an avid promoter of the Gaelic Athletic Association. He took us to his room to give the usual punishment, which was six slaps with a large strap around the back of the legs.

One of my friends in those days was Patrick Sweeney, from Fanad, which was a soccer stronghold like my own village. We had been through this type of punishment before, and knew what was coming as the priest led the parade of about ten players across the pathway to his room one evening.

Sweeney and I diverted towards the changing rooms, and quickly inserted football stockings down the legs of our pants to cushion the blow. When it came to Sweeney's turn for the strap, two dirty socks protruded visibly from the top of his pants. This seemed so obvious to everyone except the priest, who was intent on strapping us.

As Sweeney was being belted with the strap across the top of his legs, he jumped around the room after every slap, screaming as if it was extremely painful. This helped those of us who followed, as by the time 'The Doc', as we named the vice-president, had finished running around the room after Sweeney he was exhausted.

Corporal punishment was common in those days. While cruel, it seems to me important that we do not judge our teachers too harshly but that we judge them against the standards of the time. Having said that, I still have a much higher regard for those teachers, both in secondary school and primary school, who had the courage and good sense to stand apart and refrain from the use of the strap, and bullyboy tactics.

One of the things I have realised in writing this book is that many of the friendships made years ago, at secondary boarding school, have stood the test of time. I have kept in touch with classmates like Patrick Sweeney and Phonsie Gallagher over the years. Others, like Manus Ward and Mick McGinley, were not only classmates but teammates in Gaelic football. We played for the college and as county minors.

Having gone to the seminary and then worked in Scotland as a young priest for eleven years, I lost touch for awhile with these men but it was easy to resume our friendship. It has amazed me that some of the relationships formed in those early days resumed to be part of my life at a later stage. For example, Manus Ward was an excellent chief officer for the North West Health Board when we were opening the White Oaks Centre for Addicts, and was most supportive in getting this excellent service in place.

Mick McGinley, despite his son Paul's fame as an international golfer, is down to earth and has never forgotten his Donegal roots. Mick and I often laugh about another funny event from college days, which occurred one harvest night when Sweeney and I were strolling around the walks after supper and spotted Dr Cunnea and a group of his science students.

They were star gazing with the help of a large, old fashioned telescope, which was protruding from the window of a student's room. Each bedroom contained a *vas nocturum* – a tin pot for 'pee' commonly known as a 'Charlie'. We lowered the pot unto the viewing area by attaching a spool of thread to the handle. A new planet descended from above unto the viewing area!

We joked with the science class next day about the new planet, or flying saucer, which was discovered that night. The prank required a hasty retreat into the tower room. We were just in time, as the Doc scrambled up the stairs only to find an open window, but all other traces of life had gone. All went quiet as he returned to his class.

Then, of course, we had to break another rule. Knowing the priest would be waiting for us at the bottom of the students' stairway, we went down the main stairway and managed to get into last study on time.

The sheer joy of beating the system and having some fun helped us to cope with the humdrum schedule in such a boarding school.

Only a few of our peers at national, or primary, school got the opportunity to get a secondary education in the early fifties, in the Republic of Ireland. A few from Gaelic-speaking areas got scholarships, while our parents paid for the rest of us. In many ways, because my family had a business in the Waterside area of Derry, my siblings and I were among the privileged few in our primary school to get an opportunity of secondary education.

However, I was conscious of not having much knowledge of the Irish language, and of coming from a school with a poor tradition of learning. Whether it came from the teachers or elsewhere, I felt at a distinct disadvantage. At secondary school, my teacher of Irish was also my religion teacher. He was genuinely puzzled that while I got barely forty per cent in my Irish examination, I got over ninety per cent in religion. When I answered him by saying it was because I was interested in religion, he did not seem very impressed. He was from the Gaeltacht and spoke Gaelic fluently.

However, as can often be the case, it also gave me the impetus and drive to succeed and, as the years went by, I went on to achieve BA and MA degrees with some ease. I later got a distinction in the Diploma in Education at Strawberry Hill College, London, where I did teacher training, specialising in religion, with physical education as a second subject. On reflection, I got a distinction because I had worked hard, as I was not at all confident about getting a simple pass.

I did much better in education in later years than earlier, largely because of using the medium of English, and also because of being interested in the subject and voluntarily choosing the studies as an adult. Indeed, with all the faults in our seminary training I have no doubt about the benefits of the quiet times we spent in meditation, or reflection, each day, albeit we may not have fully appreciated that then.

Also, while we joke nowadays about the philosophy studies and how little we learned, I am convinced that we were at least learning to think in concepts and, while we may not have consciously realised it, we were being given a sound grounding in logic.

In getting older, I have come to accept St Paul's phrase that 'all things work together unto good for those who love God'. I very much doubt if my understanding and compassion for addicts to alcohol, and their families, would be there without my experience of some of this in my own home. Indeed, I often encourage people in recovery by pointing out that White Oaks Rehabilitation Centre would not exist were it not for my father's drinking. God will take good out of evil.

This is why we speak of the cross as a *Felix culpa*, a 'happy fault'. In some ways *Felix culpa* could easily be the title of this book, the story of my life and others. However, another title could be 'Strength in Weakness' to highlight that it is God's Power in our weakness that brings good. It is when we wait on Him and allow His will to happen that He turns evil into good. So the title, *They that Wait on the Lord*, which speaks of listening to the Lord and receiving the power of the Spirit, is the message of this book. As individuals, or as the barque of the Church on its journey, we have the Lord to guide us. The question is, are we listening, are we hearing?

The real meaning of listening to and following the Lord's will is summed up in the concept of obedience. Sadly, this word, like the word 'power', has been so often misused that it has lost its good meaning. The word obedience comes from two Latin words, *ob*, meaning towards, and *audire*, which means to hear. Towards hearing obviously means listening and, therefore, obedience for Christians entails listening to the Lord.

Sport has its place

In my youth I loved football and athletics. When I played for Carndonagh in the under sixteen age group, we won the Donegal County Juvenile Final, and I went on to play minor Gaelic football for Donegal at under eighteen level.

One area I excelled in was athletics. I remember getting the surprise of my life when I won the mile race at the annual sports in college. I was sixteen years old and in my third year. I won it again in fourth year, and this was a great confidence booster. In fact, it was noticeable, at least to me, that the attitudes of both fellow pupils and staff changed towards me after that, and academic progress at other subjects followed.

Years later, I watched a film entitled *Kes*. It was the story of a young English boy who showed no interest in education or in the boring Physical Education classes. One day he watched a kestrel fly into a tree to feed its young. He got interested in having such a bird trained, and was seen in the library reading up on the subject of kestrels. The film is used in teacher training colleges to encourage new teachers to engage in, what they term, 'pupil centred education'.

Later on, when I became a qualified teacher, the lesson of all that experience became invaluable. There is no better psychology with which to deal with needy pupils than that learned by bitter experience. Acknowledging the talents of others, be they pupils, fellow workers or employees, and promoting that, is important in building Christian community and in character building.

Looking at my brothers and sisters, some more academically schooled than others, I can see that they are all intelligent, somewhat driven and hard working. When we rightly define intelligence as 'the sum total of all a person's abilities', then we tend to hold people in proper esteem.

The sad reality has often been, however, that many teachers, often priest teachers in the old secondary schools who were unsuited to teach, were more a hindrance to pupil development than a help. The psychological marks left on pupils affected them adversely, when experience of schooling could easily have been such a pleasant one. More recently, the diverse gifts and interests of pupils are being respected and encouraged, as everyone is not suited to rote learning.

On the subject of rote learning, my view now is that we became overly pupil centred rather than subject centred in educating children. In recent times, this, applied to religion, has resulted in many pupils leaving school without knowing the Ten Commandments, not to mention other guides to help with boundaries and good behaviour.

With the introduction of a bill on abortion in the Republic recently, we had a few discussions with our congregations after the healing Masses at St Anthony's Retreat Centre, and I was surprised by the low level of information on moral teaching.

I suspect that Donegal is no different in its level of knowledge among a cross section than any other part of rural Ireland. Whether it has been the poor teaching, parenting, or lack of clear directives from the pulpit, is hard to say. For example, many thought that it was the recent Irish Government who first introduced the idea that the mother's life was to be the priority in the case of danger to the life of the child and mother in a difficult pregnancy. Few knew about the traditional moral church teaching on 'the act of two effects', as we termed it in the seminary.

However, that is another subject and this book is about my own experience in building Christian community over the past fifty years, and learning to listen to the Holy Spirit, especially in the latter stage of my life.

The Ploughed Field

As a child I watched with wonder,
as the ploughman walked all day
behind the ploughing horses.
The furrows were straight.
They were cut like sliced pan bread,
in parallel lines of equal breadth.
There, in the 'Lagan' of East Donegal,
The shiny, black, rich earth
already promised life in abundance, growth and healthy crops.

The field was, in a way, the ploughman's canvas.
He was merely marking it with the first layer of paint.
The harrows would follow and the seed
and the rollers would complete the picture.
We followed the horses as they plodded their steady way,
Up and down the landscape, not distracted by the seagulls
as they circled and landed in search of worms and food in plenty.
Those were the days before pesticide killed off
the insects and worms
that had their role to play.

These Clydesdale horses were an unlikely pair.
One was small, dark and strong,
and contrasted with the tall, brown and leaner companion.
Yet, they worked well as a team.
In perfect pace they stamped and stepped,

and turned with the skill of a couple in a dance.
I wondered how they remembered from spring to autumn,
and performed their drill again for the harvest.

Those were the days when harmony between the horses and
ploughman fascinated our young minds,
as much as the computer game today seems to occupy the youth.
Those were the days when my brother and I
could think of nothing more pleasant to do,
on a cold, early, spring Saturday morning,
than to walk beside the ploughman
and wonder where the gulls came from,
as we had not known then where the nearest seashore was.

The Past as Present

Misty water coloured memories of the way we were.

Last summer, I stopped to shop at Bradley's,
near the village of Fahan.
As I returned to my car, the distant sunset
over Rathmullan caught my eye.
The calm beauty of the golden sun's reflection
on the waters of Lough Swilly suddenly transported me,
in memory and emotion,
back to those early childhood days
of my youth at Fahan.
The mood of carefree summer evenings
for a short while returned.
Indeed, these now remain forever
stamped upon my mind and feelings.
The memory captivates a time without much responsibility,
a time before we wore wrist watches
or carried pocket diaries.
It was simply the joy of three months' summer holidays at
home and away from secondary boarding school.
I thought of rowing boats, fishing, football
and running along the golden strand.
For awhile, leaning over my car and gazing on the calm waters,
the busy schedule of the day was forgotten.
These beautiful moments are memories to behold.

These are treasures to be taken from one's memory bank
and contemplated with wonder
and with deep gratitude.
These graced moments,
captivated by the camera of one's eye and memory,
live forever.
For surely, true mindfulness is when we are really present
to nature and to our experiences.
These pictures of today and yesterday
are so much part of our soul
that they help shape us into what we are.

The Influence of Sport

With three months' summer holidays away from college, and later the seminary, it was important to me to have hobbies, such as athletics, football, hunting and fishing.

In the late fifties and early sixties, both the Gaelic Athletic Association (GAA) and the National Athletic and Cycling Association (NACA) had a strict amateur status; members could not compete for financial reward. This had implications for those of us who loved football and athletics, and who also wanted to earn our few pounds' pocket money during the summer, so that we could be somewhat financially independent.

I was a member of the Oak Leaf Athletic Club in Derry for some years, and competed at events in the county and in Belfast. We won the Ulster Clubs' Athletics Championship in 1960, and went on to represent Ulster against the Connaught winners, Galway, at Ballina that summer.

I remember running in, and often winning, events at sports days throughout Co. Donegal as an eighteen- or nineteen-year-old student. The Oak Leaf Club had strict rules on amateur status that officially prohibited members from running for prize money, or competing at ordinary parish sports days around the country. Often, the money prizes were generous so, as a clerical student with three months' holidays and no income, I ran under another name, that of my uncle, Patsy Breslin, who lived in Derry. In this way, I was able to keep myself in pocket money.

The sports became a very attractive and lucrative business, but we were always on the lookout for zealous members of NACA, and the officials from the Oak Leaf Athletic Club in particular, as some felt obliged to report others to the Club's committee for running at these 'flapper' meetings.

On one occasion, I recall standing in the sports field in Milford, Co. Donegal, at nine o'clock at night waiting for a lift in a van to Letterkenny. That morning I had travelled over from Fahan on a boat and then cycled from Rathmullan to Milford. After running all day and winning a number of events, I got talking to a man who told me that I had won the equivalent to one week's wages for an ordinary labourer – eight punts, or pounds in those days.

Eventually, it was discovered that I was running under the name 'P. Breslin' and, together with George Williamson, another athlete from Derry, I was banned from participating in amateur athletics for a year. This was my first experience of excommunication.

Prior to our expulsion from the ranks of the NACA, we had lots of fun competing at local sports meetings. I remember, on one occasion, lining up with at least twenty others to run a two hundred and twenty yards' race. For the uninitiated, that involved running around a curve. The challenge was all the more difficult as there were no lanes to run in, and the starter complicated matters further with his instructions before the race. Normally, the starter in such a race as this would say, 'On your marks. Get set' and then shoot a cap gun. However, this particular starter told us that he would say, 'On your marks. Get set' and then drop a handkerchief, but we were not to run until the handkerchief hit the ground.

I was on the extreme outside of the group. My friend, Jimmy Logue, who was a prominent member of the Oak Leaf Athletic Club and, like me, should not have been running at these sports, was placed well on the inside of this large group of runners.

As I was a middle distance runner and Jimmy was a sprinter, I figured that this race required tactics. Jimmy and I looked over at each other and smiled knowingly, as we both knew exactly what was going to happen.

The starter said, 'On your marks' and we took off! We were not going to wait around for the other nonsense. I reached the corner first, but only just. There was a good sprinter from Churchill, Willie Devine, whose spikes caught the hard sole of my spikes after ripping down through the soft leather, cutting my left foot. I felt the ground literally shake under my feet as about eighteen bodies hit the earth behind me with an almighty thud. Two of us finished that race. Jimmy came second and I came first. We both talked about this particular sports event many years later, but Jimmy could not remember the race. I suggested to him that he had a selective memory.

Afterwards, I got attention from the Irish Red Cross for my injury, but it did not stop me lining up for the four hundred and forty yards race shortly afterwards. I still have the mark of that spike on my left foot. The price of success, or the cost of discipleship!

As I write about these happy memories of the sports days, I look out at the same white strand where, as a young man, I ran and trained almost daily. I owe much to athletics and football. Indeed, as a young priest in the sixties when, in changing times, many of my colleagues were leaving the priesthood, I was helped in my vocation, and in life's journey, by the discipline and interest athletics demanded. The sheer joy of running and feeling fit, after running at six-thirty in the morning, made my priestly duty of visiting easy, whether to homes, hospital or schools.

If I were to develop a new religious order for young men in these times, I would look to gather those interested in athletics and in physical fitness, as well as in the life of prayer. If ever a nation needed a health dimension to be emphasised in the formation of clerics, then Ireland does.

Let us hold out this as a vision for some of tomorrow's youth who are keen on sport, and who also seek to serve and build up God's Kingdom. Perhaps, it was with this in mind that I included a running track in my first plans for White Oaks Rehabilitation Centre for recovering addicts. A healthy mind in a healthy body, as the old saying goes.

I write this chapter with some realisation of how important exercise has been in my life. I am seventy-three years of age and recently had the privilege of winning the Derry Diocesan clergy annual golf tournament for the third successive year. It was a beautiful day and the company was good also.

It is amazing what we learn about each other on the golf course. Virtues and faults are on display, whether we are conscious of it or not. Unlike the starter's rules at Milford sports, the rules of golf are such that the player's honesty and sense of fairness are encouraged.

Someone involved in spiritual direction pointed out to me that the game of golf involves focus, and the power to live in the present. No matter how the previous shot or, indeed, the previous hole went, the present shot or putt for the hole was the one that mattered.

This mentality is remarkably like the spirituality of those who teach the importance of living in the present moment, and the power of now. Whether we prefer the modern term, 'mindfulness', or good old contemplative, or centring, prayer, the effect of stillness has to have positive outcomes. It is about living in the present. This is also the philosophy, or spirituality, underlying the Alcoholics Anonymous movement for the healing of addicts. There, it is referred to as 'living one day at a time'.

We can do little or nothing about the past. We may have some little influence on shaping the future under God's direction. All we can do is live in the present and, by listening, we can give the present our best shot.

This is one of the hardest things that people with high anxiety levels need to learn to do. To just sit, breathe easily, and develop awareness and consciousness, is not alone a great help to our physical and mental health, it is also essential for any Christian prayer life and meditation. It is part of allowing Jesus to be Lord, and a prerequisite for listening and healthy decision making. This is not only true for those involved in church leadership, but for all baptised as children of God. If Jesus found it necessary to spend time aside in quiet consultation with the Father, then we, His followers, are called to imitate that.

I am aware that this last paragraph has promoted reflection and prayer, though this chapter is about sport and its influence in my life, but, the fact is, I have consistently associated both as an integrated whole. Life is in many parts, and all are meant to complement each other for the glory of God.

To this end, I recall being at a Better World Retreat in the late sixties at Coodham House, in Kilmarnock, Scotland. For the offertory procession at the final Mass, the priest requested us to take up something that had a special place in our lives. These were to symbolise our gifts and our readiness, not only to give thanks, but also our willingness to give our lives to God.

Some brought bibles, or photographs of their profession or ordination. I immediately went to my car boot and got my running spikes as a symbol of athletics, which had played such a key role in my life and formation from when I was a young man. Indeed, that particular year I was twenty eight years of age and had just run my fastest time for the four hundred metres, of forty nine point three seconds.

After retiring from playing Gaelic football at thirty-five years of age, I continued to jog on the beach into my fifties. Now I walk a little and play golf. The joints suffer somewhat, and the effects of operations on the knee, and on the foot, take their toll.

However, I have no regrets due to over-exercise. It has been a great gift. Even now, to watch running and football on television is a delight, as I appreciate the effort and training that has gone into such achievements.

Having said all that, it seems to me that the emphasis on winning has become part and parcel of the GAA games and, at times, this can verge on the fanatical. Sport is in danger of becoming the new religion, and replacing the priority and emphasis we put on church attendance in our young days.

If Elijah, the leading prophet, were to return to visit God's people, I suspect that he would have some words of advice to offer the worshippers of the 'Baal' or the Ball today. In our days as altar boys in Newtown, we did not dare to play football in the park while Devotions were happening on a Sunday afternoon or during May and October Devotions. We were all expected to attend prayer times, whether we were servers or not.

While it is accepted that the church had a heavy hand on society in those days, it must be said that youth and adult behaviour has apparently not progressed during the so-called liberal times we are experiencing. As the old axiom goes, virtue lies in the middle.

A good balance between sport and other social agencies that help form good character needs to be agreed to and promoted.

The White Strand at Fahan

The flow of the tide,
the gentle glow of the sun,
the quiet breeze upon my face,
the crackle of the sea shells
beneath the sharp spikes of the running shoes
we wore in those days gone by.

Today, as I muse upon these sensations,
it seems like a well-conducted chorus
of sounds and feelings
playing in rhythm.
They pay tribute to a full life led.
They recall the days of joy, of athletics, of fishing.
We sat quietly along the sand hills near the beach,
listening for the white trout to jump at night,
or to splash and dip the net.

The elements of air, sea, sand and shell
awake beautiful memories
of the sheltered place we call Fahan.
It seems to me that our fun and joy were united
with the men of prayer,
who sanctified this ancient, monastic place
with their psalms sung day and night
to glorify the king,
the Lord of land and sea
and of all people.

The Seminary and Ordination

I left secondary school in 1958 and entered the seminary at St Peter's College, in Wexford. In those days, in Ireland, there were few career choices put before us other than the serving vocations, such as teaching, medicine or priesthood.

In fact, few spoke about careers at all. There was an ethos in all the minor seminaries – the boarding schools in each diocese – which was conducive to fostering a student's interest in religion, and I found great comfort in that.

Our peer group influenced us in these matters more than the staff did. I remember, for example, getting into the habit of saying the Rosary before going to sleep at night after being told by a friend, Phonsie Gallagher, that this was his nightly routine.

Visiting the Blessed Sacrament in the chapel, during the short break from study after six o'clock in the evening, was another habit we practiced together. On reflection, these religious exercises which were done voluntarily were the ones that really mattered. The other daily religious exercises that we were obliged to do, like attending daily prayers and daily Mass, did not seem to involve the same type of character building, though I am sure they also had a positive influence when participated in wholeheartedly.

So, when it came to choosing a career, or vocation, I have to say that I was greatly influenced by fellow pupils and their decision to go into seminaries, though my two closest friends and I chose three different seminaries. After a few years, the two of them left their seminaries and later chose other successful careers, got married and raised families.

Going into the senior seminary at eighteen years of age, in the south east of Ireland, may have seemed a strange decision to my friends. After all, we spent the entire summer holidays playing football, running at athletic meetings, and going to dances at least twice a week.

I remember telling a neighbour, who was wondering why I was going to the seminary, that I felt obliged by God to go, but that He may well tell me that He wants me elsewhere after a year or two!

I felt strange during the first few holidays from the senior seminary. I did not act like the few seminarians from the next parish, who were all trained in Maynooth. Back then, those in other seminaries were destined to minister outside the Irish diocesan system.

I do not recall meeting local clerical students then who would have previously gone to dances, or shown interest in girls as I had as a young man. I wondered if a real vocation to priesthood somehow consisted in either not having such attractions or a readiness to deny this affective side of my nature.

Indeed, this has been a lifelong question, and only gradually have I become more comfortable with celibacy and relationships with others. I sense that relationships developed in the Columba Community have contributed greatly to my own development. It seems to me that, psycho-sexually, some young priests need help if they are to mature, and become reasonably balanced, and fit, for ministry of the variety they find themselves involved in.

While running at sports meetings and playing football with the local Gaelic football team occupied me during vacations, it was still a lonely time when, in my father's words, 'you are neither fish nor flesh'; neither priest nor lay person. Luckily, we lived by the sea at Fahan and I spent time hunting, fishing and shooting with local lads from Inch Island.

The seminary was not a place that appealed to me. I had some difficult times there, finding it such a rigid system with little room for divergent thinkers. There was little emphasis on academic achievement at St Peter's, which later seemed to spur some of us on to do further studies in areas of interest.

Spiritually speaking, I recall a devotion to the Stations of the Cross. Somehow, that devotion hooked me and was a prayerful exercise that appealed to my spirit. I have often asked myself why that was. Perhaps my own, and others', sufferings had something to do with it. The sense of faith in the power of the cross as the answer to the quest for happiness was, even then, strong in my thinking. If Christ's death was so central to Christianity, then it seemed right to wonder how that affected me.

Later in my life, a deeper spiritual awakening was to occur which helped to answer that question. The greater significance of the death and resurrection of the Christ, and His role as living Lord of my life, was something that would happen for me much later.

From an early age, I was extremely shy, and that shyness has never quite disappeared. The freedom and self-worth that came later, following my Baptism in the Spirit when I asked for the release of the gifts already received in the Sacrament of Baptism, certainly caused a big change in my life.

As time passed, I enjoyed the friendships in the seminary, and the football twice weekly was a lifesaver. My fellow Wexford students could not have been friendlier. They formed an ideal community spirit for those of us coming from all over the island, even if we took some time to understand what on earth each other was saying, such was the mix of diverse accents.

Study

There was no great emphasis in the seminary on reading outside the course. Indeed, there was not even a decent library. Academic development consisted in taking copious notes in class, be they on subjects like scholastic philosophy, scripture, or on moral and dogmatic theology, and reproducing these verbatim at examination times, or during 'hat calls' or orals.

The 'hat call' was when, each month or so, the lecturer would call a name at random. One time my colleague, Michael Collins from Co. Cork, was called. He stood up while asking me to get a book open. This little book gave a very clear summary of the course in Dogma we were studying. Dr Sherwood asked Mick some obscure question to which I could not find the answer and of which Mick was totally ignorant.

Mick, I should add, was a brilliant student and had seven honours in his leaving certificate prior to entering the seminary. He stood tall and said, as only he would, 'I'm afraid, Father, I cannot recall all the exact details in answer to that particular question at the moment.' We and Dr Sherwood laughed, of course, which was the desired response Mick wanted. He spent his final years of ministry in Florida, where he sadly died in 2012.

I recall the experience of another classmate during an oral exam. The president, dean and relevant lecturer were present at this. The student, Paddy, was asked a difficult question, to which he made no response. It was springtime and the windows of the lecture hall were open. In the deafening silence, one could hear the sound of the cattle, in clear rhythm, munching lush grass outside, on what was supposed to be a lawn. These were cheap lawnmowers in those days. Paddy, in silence, gazed out the window, looking totally unconcerned for what seemed to be a long time. Finally, the philosophy professor, said: 'It's a nice day Mr Byrne.' Paddy retorted: 'It is, Father', and the silence resumed for ages. All the time, Paddy looked very relaxed and did not even look our way for a signal or an answer. Eventually, he was told to return to his place.

Speaking to Paddy afterwards, as we stood out at the famous gate having a smoke, I asked him how come he was so relaxed about it all, as the set up was geared to create the utmost of tension. He said: 'The minute I got that question I realised I knew nothing about that subject. Had I known anything at all, I would have wracked my mind trying to answer, however, when I knew nothing I just decided to relax.'

That may well have been the case, but the fact that Paddy had already decided to leave the seminary at that point surely played a major part in his carefree response.

There was a lot of time spent in the chapel but I, for one, was not guided in how to pray or how to listen to God. This lack of proper formation, and feeling of not being ready to be spiritual directors, was the sense most students had. When we later looked back, reflecting on our formation and sharing our thoughts, my fellow students and I agreed that we learned a lot on the job, thanks to our good parishioners and family support.

Healthy and Unhealthy Obedience
In the seminary, we were supposed to believe that the will of God would always be revealed to us if we listened to our superiors. They were to be the voice of God to us. One day, our president arrived at the chapel quite annoyed, due to some incident. He told us: 'The Pope is guided by God. He tells the bishops what to do. The bishops tell us what to do in the seminary training and you, as students, just obey!' He then walked out. I was totally puzzled as to what he was referring to, but later gathered that there had been a request from senior students to change some rules of the seminary.

What if we are taught to obey authority blindly and that an authority figure, for example Hitler, tells us to obey him blindly? We know from the trials at Nuremberg that some German army officers and private soldiers used this blind obedience to authority argument, in the hope that the judges would excuse them from being responsible for their part in the terrible atrocities of the Holocaust. It did not work then, nor should it ever, as we are each equipped with free will and must, in the final analysis, answer to God and our conscience.

Experiments on students in an American university in the sixties gave us some startling insights. It was entitled 'The Milgram Experiment'. I recall this from my days studying sociology. The leading lecturer conducted an experiment whereby he ordered some of his students to inflict degrees of pain on a selection of subjects, in order to get them to answer questions more promptly. The students were instructed, at the command of the renowned professor, to press buttons which would inflict not only severe pain but also possible fatal levels of electricity to some clients. To the amazement of other members of staff, an alarming percentage of these students were ready to inflict severe pain and even kill in obedience to the highly reputable authority. This example tells us how immoral it is to blindly obey. Fortunately, the subjects of the experiment were professional actors, who pretended to be in various levels of pain and, in some cases, even pretended to pass out.

Yet, we need to respect those in authority in all walks of life. Good order requires this, and listening with respect to the wisdom of parents and elders, and those who are tasked with leadership, is generally a good thing. That should be part of our discernment process of what obedience really means.

It seems important to say that the word 'obedience' comes from the words *ob* meaning towards and *audire* meaning hearing.

Towards hearing certainly implies listening. Listening to the Spirit of truth is surely the ultimate. That we need order, and someone to be in charge in the Church, is basic, yet without listening to God's Spirit in leadership, without a discerning community who 'hear God's will when I listen', to quote Colmcille, we have no right to wield authority over people, or set ourselves up as guides or shepherds. Jesus did what he saw the Father do, and said only what the Father told him to say. The best shepherds are guided by discernment gained from prayer, and listening to the Spirit in the signs of the times.

As it states in the Gospel of Mark, 1:22, 'His teaching made a deep impression on them because, unlike the scribes, he taught them with authority'. The authority here is the ability to inspire and encourage people to listen to a pure, still voice within, which we call a healthy conscience.

Jesus instilled confidence in people so that they knew God loved them and that they were precious in his eyes. They knew they were important to God, and when they heard Jesus speak they knew, from the Spirit of truth within them, that He was close to God.

To listen to God, who speaks to hearts through His Spirit, is the way forward. It requires prayer, and awareness that God also desires the deepest and purest desire of the heart.

Rules and punishment
The journey of six years in the seminary had its ups and downs. I was one of six students from the Donegal area to reside at St Peter's in those days. I remember being invited by one of them to come to the dark room – the photography room – one day during Easter week, which follows Holy week. There we shared some chocolate, a forbidden fruit in those days. They called such sweets and cakes, 'contraband'. Little did I realise then that this

forbidden fruit would have such a dire effect on our lives in the seminary!

A few days later, the dean came to my room asking for the names of all those who had attended that party. I admitted that I had broken the rule and ate contraband. When I told him that I thought it would not be right to tell on others, he said that he knew their names anyway. When I said that I would let him know if he got all of them or not if he mentioned the names, he seemed annoyed. I suspect that conversation goes some way to explaining why my call to minor orders was delayed over the following few years.

That experience was capped by another incident which almost got me expelled altogether. You will know by now that athletics played a major part in my life, so when I got a bad foot injury before sports day in my first year, and had to sit it out and watch the events from the bench, you will appreciate that it was a painful experience for me in a couple of ways.

I wondered what the Lord was teaching me, as I had just sprained the foot the previous day while playing basketball. Jumping for a ball, I landed awkwardly on the foot of the player who was to be my main opponent in the mile race the following day. He won the race easily. Watching that race and knowing I could have won it, made me wonder was I being taught patience and, yet again, being asked to get my priorities right.

The following year I won the mile and a few other events to win the Victor Ludorum – 'the winner of the games'. When the sports were over, I felt very sick and unable to stop vomiting. During the night that chronic sickness continued. I distinctly recall thinking that I would be happy to throw all the prizes on my table out the window just for one hour's ease or sleep.

Not having slept, I contacted my friend next door in the morning, and asked him to report to the nursing sister-in-charge that I was ill. However, instead of a visit from the sister who looked after the sick, the president of the seminary arrived ranting and raving to my room, demanding that I get up immediately and go to the dining room. I staggered a bit on arising, but made my way to the dining room, though I was unable to eat or drink. Even the lights in that otherwise dark room were difficult to endure those days.

Shortly after that, the dean called me up and accused me of breaking a rule which stated that 'No student shall absent himself without permission from the general body between night prayer and morning prayer.' When I stated that I was so sick that the rule was not uppermost in my mind, it was no excuse. The scene was set.

About two weeks later, a few of us were presented individually before the staff council. The offence was read out and the president gave the last warning, asking if I had anything to say. I recall vividly glancing down at the staff. A Fr Tom Sherwood shook his head as a warning, and I agreed to say nothing. After that incident, my call to receive the minor rights, which clerics get on their way to ordination, was postponed for a year.

I do not stand alone in my disappointment in the system of election of presidents that prevailed in the seminary. Some were totally unsuited. Priests, either by training or by nature, were often not ready to challenge the status quo, even when it was obviously abusive and wrong. This is something that requires attention, if we are to understand how we have reached the present state as a Catholic Church in Ireland.

During the week leading up to my ordination, I received minor orders, sub-deaconate and deaconate. No wonder the ordaining prelate, exiled Archbishop of Nancheng, China, Patrick Cleary, whispered to me: 'I have seen a lot of you this week. Keep it up.'

I have never forgotten that moment of human affirmation and the smile of that Columban priest, who was exiled from China in the mid-fifties. He had his priorities right. The petty rules we were punished for breaking in the seminary, such as talking or eating a sweet, would fall into proper perspective when viewed by a good missionary priest like Archbishop Cleary, after a lifetime in China.

There were fourteen of us ordained together on 31 May 1964 by Archbishop Cleary, as the local bishop in the Ferns Diocese at the time, Bishop Staunton, had died the previous year. While some were to serve in the home diocese, others had chosen to go abroad to America, England or Scotland. I chose Scotland.

My three sisters, six brothers and my parents travelled to Wexford for my ordination. My memory of that day was one of gratitude, and relief that I had survived the seminary, together with a sense of wonder as to what the future held.

Coming home to Donegal to say my first Mass in St Mura's Church, in Fahan, I was somewhat shocked at the bonfires and welcome. Given the sense of being cut off from the social life of the local community, which I had felt as a student during the holidays, I was surprised at what the ordination of a local boy meant to the people.

I had only come to the home parish of Fahan as a boarding school student of thirteen, when my family had moved there from another village, so I did not get the chance to meet many of the locals, that is, with the exception of the footballers on Inch Island.

While I was happy to be ordained, I must say that it was a strange feeling. There I was, with a group of others, now suddenly ordained. Somehow, we were to act differently and do functions, preach and administer sacraments, which we had never done before. I felt that I was someone else, and was not sure if I could be myself and be this person called 'priest' at the same time. In a way, that has been the situation ever since.

It is a call to go beyond where human nature takes us, and, in that sense, we do not have a choice but to seek a power greater than ourselves. If the life of the Christian, never mind the priest, is to be led happily and fully then, indeed, the life of the Holy Spirit needs to be allowed to guide and inspire us in all kinds of ways.

In that sense, I can say that, until I experienced the Baptism in the Holy Spirit some ten years after my ordination, life for me was lived in my own willpower. It was an active life. I was active with parish and school work, youth clubs and athletic clubs, during those early and, generally, very happy days in the Motherwell Diocese, in Scotland.

Reflection

After looking back on my time in the seminary, I want to say that some good formation took place as well.

We were supposed to be getting prepared for diocesan work all over the English-speaking world. However, for some I knew, who had arrived in inner cities on the west coast of America, it became a question of learning on the hoof and relying heavily on one's colleagues.

One friend of mine later compared his induction to downtown Orlando to the scene from *The Deer Hunter* movie, where Robert De Niro and his friends are, one minute, at a dance in their country town in Pennsylvania, and the next minute are suddenly being landed by military helicopter as soldiers in the centre of the jungle of Vietnam, amid the turmoil of machine gunfire. A bit dramatic perhaps, but in those days of little or no television, arriving from rural Ireland to a strange culture certainly proved challenging.

What kept our hopes up was the sense of new expectations in the air in the early sixties, and what was promised by the Vatican Council, then still in session. The talk about the vernacular, ecumenism, lay participation in both liturgy and governance of the church, and the prayer for a new Pentecost, which Pope John XXIII had us all say at that time, were all signs of good things to come.

In those days of more openness and change, there was also talk of optional celibacy, which was misleading and contributed towards expectations, and the large numbers who would later leave the priesthood to get married.

Shortly after we left St Peter's Seminary in 1964, the regime changed quite quickly. Students were suddenly treated like adults. They were allowed to venture downtown at the least excuse, and made up their own minds regarding attendance at daily Mass and other exercises. That was an overreaction.

However, later still, there was a return to more sensible rules and regulations. The attempt to reform the training was too late, by and large. St Peter's and all the provincial seminaries have closed down over the past twenty years due to a lack of vocations. This was on the cards. Anyone who looked at society in Ireland in the sixties, and since then, would easily understand that the regime we knew was light years away from the emerging society we were supposed to be in touch with.

While I have nothing against praying for vocations to the priesthood for those who can abide by the rules, especially the celibacy rule, it seems to me that the God who speaks to us through the signs of the times is shouting to the church leaders about getting really serious on the training of the laity for all kinds of ministry.

It is strange that in dioceses up and down the country, where there seemed to be plenty of money to educate students for priesthood, there has not been money for the development of lay ministry.

Even with laity receiving qualifications at places like All Hallows College, there have not been the employment opportunities one would expect in these days of dire need for new life in the church.

While it is good to highlight these issues in the hope that people of influence may do something about them, doing our best to offer a model of the way forward has always been the work of members of Columba Community.

To be what we are,
to become what we are capableof becoming,
is the only end in life.

Life in Scotland

As a twenty-four-year-old newly-ordained priest, I arrived in Scotland in July 1964 and was appointed to St Cuthbert's Parish, in Burnbank, Hamilton, Lanarkshire. I met some great people in Scotland, where I ministered for the first eleven years, apart from a year spent at Strawberry Hill Teacher Training College, in London, in 1970.

Shortly after arriving, I was delighted to meet up with a school friend of mine, Gerry Devenney, who had left Ireland to work in Scotland when he was just seventeen years of age. On Sunday evenings after Mass, I would drive into Glasgow to visit Gerry and his wife, Ann, and their young children. It was a time of fun and jokes and sometimes we would go to the films.

The fact that Ann also came from near my home in Fahan added to the sense of belonging experienced there. This friendship has lasted a lifetime. Now, Gerry is retired and the couple spend much of their time in Donegal. The meetings, meals, games of golf and conversations, through good times and times of trial, have helped to sustain us in life.

I have noticed over the years that a large percentage of Donegal people who spent their time working in Scotland and, in many cases, reared their families there, seem to have retained their faith, and become quite involved in their local parish. Whether this was because they saw the local Sunday Mass as their connection with the values they had learned at home, or that it was simply a social meeting place, is hard to say.

Perhaps it was both but they certainly seemed proud to belong to St John's or St Eunan's or St Dominic's, depending on what area of Glasgow they came from. Unlike in Ireland, when you asked Catholics in the west of Scotland where they came from, they answered by giving the name of the Church as well as the town they came from. There was a pride in belonging to the faith community. I wonder is it still the same today?

My day off was spent with fellow Irish priests I had known in the seminary, who had also come to work in Scotland. We would have an hour's car journey to and from the golf course, and we often enjoyed that trip as much as the game. In those carefree days of youth we did not take our golf too seriously. We certainly enjoyed the fun and each other's company.

Later, I missed that weekly trip and company due to teacher training, and then school work. For some reason, I did not take a day off when I was chaplain or teaching in school, even though that was followed by a very busy weekend schedule of Masses. I eventually got sick from this busy schedule. Since then, no matter how busy or important the work schedule, I always advocate a day off for fellow clergy, even if I fail some weeks to abide by this myself.

Visiting the homes of parishioners was a big feature of a priest's work in those days. I visited 'The Jungle', which was a large housing estate in Burnbank, and got to know every family in my district. I recall a visit to one of the homes in a large crescent, where I spoke to a lady who had an only child – a daughter. She kept telling me how good her daughter was but gave out hell about her 'good son'. I kept wondering what the other son must be like if the 'good son' was as bad as depicted. I was very puzzled by this, as there was only one child mentioned in the little parish census book that we had. Finally, it transpired that the 'good son' was a local term for son-in-law.

There were three priests in St Cuthbert's and, unlike rural Ireland, in industrial Scotland we all lived in one house, each with a bed-sitter. It was a homely enough arrangement, where we shared meals in common. We had lunch at one o'clock and evening meal at nine o'clock, which gave us all evening to visit homes. Those were the days before evening weekday Mass began, and the Mass was in Latin.

There were a couple of unusual groups of people in Burnbank Parish. One was the small Lithuanian community living in the area and the other was the poorer native Irish group, mostly labourers, who lived in the local Model Lodging House.

The Lithuanians came to Scotland to work in the coal mines in the twenties and thirties. They were sent by train from London. Some of the original emigrants were still alive when I brought these old people Holy Communion in the mid-sixties. Some still spoke only a few words of English and said most of their prayers in their native tongue. Monthly, Fr Joe Godowsky would arrive at St Cuthbert's Church to conduct devotions, with strange sounding hymns.

One of them told me of how the men had arrived in Glasgow with a metal plate around their neck marked 'Shotts No. 2' or 'Blantyre No. 1', depending on what coal mine they were destined for. They were then allocated a home in one of the miners' rows, as they were named. The next day, at the pit entrance, they were given a new name to facilitate the administration. Instead of their original name they were renamed Brown, Black, Smith, or a similar short name. In speaking to the Browns and Smiths in the parish, I found out their real names.

Some, however, managed to retain their family names, such as the local headmaster, Mr Bansevish. These old people were highly respectful to us as priests, and were extremely devout and prayerful.

The Model Lodging House, where the Irish lived, was run by Harry Doyle, whose family was very involved in parish life. I became friendly with this family of parents and three grown up sons. Each night we would say the Rosary together with the residents, and afterwards I enjoyed a cup of tea with Harry's family.

There were a few Model Lodging Houses in industrial areas in Scotland. They consisted of inexpensive accommodation for single men, who mostly worked locally as labourers. Some were unemployed, and a small section of them had alcohol problems. Quite a number were Irish men who had come over to Scotland in the fifties. Many of them were from the west of Donegal and were quiet bachelors who wanted to keep to themselves.

I was amazed at the number of them who would turn up for the Rosary in the house every evening, and yet few of them would attend Sunday Mass in the parish, with the church only about six hundred metres from the hostel.

I went to Bishop Thomson for permission to conduct a mini-retreat in the lodging house and to offer Mass there. He was concerned that the hostel was only a short distance from the church, but I recall saying to him: 'It is a short distance in space but, psychologically, it is a long way for them to go.'

Bishop Thomson was very accommodating and wished me well with the retreat. With the help of Harry, the proprietor, the retreat, insofar as we could judge, was a great success. I have been told that this lodging house has long since gone out of use.

Looking back at those early days from my present Golden Jubilee year in the priesthood, I can see that I was always attracted to the marginalised and the poor. It is not surprising, therefore, that more than forty years later I am involved in the care of addicts, unemployed, and young people who would be labelled as low achievers.

My memories of the parish are happy ones. The founding of St Cuthbert's Athletic Club, with the help of Bob Lennon and Inspector Bob Farrell, two of a number of good policemen in our parish, was a landmark occasion. We had some fine young athletes who won many underage trophies throughout Scotland.

In brief, those early days in priesthood and ministry, visiting schools, caring for the sick, and visiting parishioners in their homes, were happy days without much sense of responsibility for 'running the plant', that is, the upkeep of parish property and looking after the finances, which was the remit of the parish priest.

Come to think of it, the parish priest was ill in Ireland when I arrived so I never did get to meet Fr Walsh, from Mayo. He died that autumn, so the senior curate was the administrator for nearly a year before being replaced by the new parish priest, Fr Barney Keegan.

Barney spoke to me the day after he arrived to let me know that he was now in charge. We got on well together. Once when visiting him, after I had left Scotland to minister in Derry, he paid me a compliment, saying: 'The good men, like you, are either going to the missions or back to Ireland.' That was one of the few compliments I recall from him. He was an honest-to-God type of quiet, Irish priest, who was respected and loved by the people.

For twenty years before coming to our parish, he had been working in a nearby mining area, and he talked about those tough times quite a bit. This interested me, as the only sign of mining left behind was the large, smoldering mounds of dust that I would pass on my early morning run on the country road overlooking Blantyre, the hometown of the explorer, David Livingston, who went to Zambia, in Africa. Little did I know then that I would visit Zambia often over the following forty years, as my sister and her husband reared their family there.

Sport continued to play a large part in my life when I went to Scotland. I was still involved with Gaelic football and athletics, and I was president of the Gaelic Athletic Association in Scotland for a few years.

I trained early every morning, ran in the highland games on a Saturday during the summer months, and often played Gaelic football on a Sunday afternoon in Glasgow, which was only a half hour trip from our parish. It was tremendous.

Good old Miss Boyle, our housekeeper used to say, as I ran out the door in my tracksuit: 'You will wear yourself out with all that running.'

I loved Gaelic football as I could give myself wholeheartedly in that game. For me, it was a sport that allowed me to express my love for both running and competitiveness.

However, having watched my young nephew play in an under fourteen game, I wonder where the emphasis on physical attacking will bring us today. It seemed to me more enjoyable when close marking and heavy tackling were not so central to the game. I think it is time to review the rules as there are far too many injuries in this amateur game now, and that is coming from someone who did not hold back a lot either.

During the summer we had track and field events at the highland games. I managed to compete in some of them around Glasgow and Edinburgh. The parish priests I had in those days were quite supportive of my participation in athletics provided, of course, that the other duties were given proper attention as well.

I can remember vividly, however, being so tired after a day of athletics that I fell asleep in the confessional box! I woke up to the sound of a woman's voice saying: 'That is all I want to confess.' Needless to say, I had to ask her to repeat her confession. Around that time I also injured my Achilles tendon while running, so it was clearly time to pack in the competitive running anyway.

I recall one Saturday afternoon coming back with a squad of young lads covered in muck and dirt, after being down at the soccer pitch, and meeting our parish priest, Fr Tom Winning, later to become Cardinal Winning. Always encouraging, he said: 'Good! These kids will remember this long after they have forgotten most of what they heard in church.'

Well I, for one, remember it, and I remember Tom and his kindness to me and members of my family, especially my mother, when she visited Scotland on the way to visit my sister in England.

While in Scotland, I also ran for a club with senior athletes in Glasgow, known as the Shettleston Harriers. Harry Doyle, a schoolteacher friend who threw the hammer for Shettleston, introduced me to the club. We enjoyed some great outings in Glasgow and Edinburgh, as well as at highland games around Scotland. Back then, in the sixties, I recall listening to the 'heavies', as we called them, the weight throwers of hammer, shot, discus and caber tossers alike, talking freely about taking anabolic steroids. Now, when I listen to the debate about drug-enhanced performances, I wonder where the regulators were in those early days of the mid-to-late-sixties.

I was persuaded by a coach to run the four hundred metres; a race I had detested from my youth, as it was neither a sprint nor a middle-distance race. I finally clocked forty nine point three seconds in this event, before giving up competitive athletics after my Achilles tendon went at Meadowbank Stadium in 1968. After that, I played football until 1976, when I was thirty-six years of age.

For most of those early years, my involvement with Gaelic, and chairing the local Gaelic Athletic Association Board in Glasgow, kept me in touch with many of the Irish diaspora. These lads met on a Sunday afternoon at Eastfield Gaelic Park, which, for many, was a place to go during their free time at weekends, as they were not encouraged to hang around the house where they had lodgings.

The vast majority of the men I met there were from Donegal, and we managed to organise three teams. Often I could only play until half-time, and then I had to rush back to my parish to offer evening Mass or Devotions on a Sunday afternoon. Energy was never a problem in those days.

Companionship

With all this talk about games and running, it seems important to mention that I was just as passionate about my faith and parish work as about sport, which should not be surprising because if I had preferred sport I could have become a physical education teacher. But we were young priests and, in those days, many of my companions were leaving the priesthood, generally to be free to meet a young woman and maybe get married. In fact, there were five ordained in my year for the diocese, three Scots and two Irish. The three Scots left within the first five years.

I really think my interest in sports, particularly in running, helped me to keep a balanced lifestyle. This is in no way to question the sincerity of the priests who left to get married. Back then, it was one thing to make a decision at eighteen to enter a seminary to be a priest and, in the sheltered environment of the college, to choose priesthood with its package deal, which includes celibacy. It is quite another thing, when alone on a Sunday evening or going for a walk, and missing the company of college friends and family, to continue to choose the single life that the priesthood demands. To want the company of a girl to share one's hopes and dreams with is the most natural thing in the world. After all, God made them male and female.

In the sixties, when we were asked to develop our humanity, to mix more with people, to become more intimate and unafraid of being part of people's lives, we were also supposed to remain celibate priests and be an eschatological sign. It required an understanding of our psycho-spiritual and sexual selves that we simply were not prepared for in the seminary training.

When they began to get in touch with their feelings of being attracted to a particular girl, many young men left the ministry. As one priest said at the time: 'I do not know yet whether I want to get married or not, but I would want to get permission at least to go out on a date!'

Maybe we could learn something from the Greek Orthodox Church on this very important issue. Then again, had we had the advantage of good spiritual direction and methods of discernment, such as that available in Ignatian exercises and spirituality, we would have been more mature and more helpful to others in matters of decision-making amid conflicting emotions.

Around that time, I became friendly with the local Methodist minister and his wife. They lived nearby and used to help me with the parish weekly news bulletin. Revd David would type up what I had written, which I then run off on a photocopier. One day, he introduced me to a twenty-year-old lady from his church who wanted to become a Catholic. I was quite amazed that he did not, in any way, try to persuade Freda to remain a Methodist, but was happy to support her on her spiritual journey. He was English and, dare I say, more ecumenical than most of the clergy that I met monthly at the local fraternity.

Freda had finished her studies in Business at Glasgow University, and had already begun to take instruction in the Catholic faith. This consisted of a weekly series of talks and notes, which lasted some six months. In brief, the instructions in the faith which many of us were involved in giving were simply the Catholic Catechism shared in conversational tone. Given the fact that we were a minority church, of some eighteen per cent of the population, it was not unusual to have mixed marriages as well as small numbers of converts each year.

Freda wanted to become a Catholic because of conviction, after reading up on the faith and finding it attractive. She was also strongly influenced by the Catholic students she had met at university. She took an active part in church life, especially as a member of the choir and our youth club for girls.

Over the weeks and months that followed our first meeting, I found myself growing fonder of her company. So much so that I stopped going into the girls' youth club, in the mistaken belief that the attraction would wear off. As I look back now, it is amazing the lengths we, as young men, would go to deny our human feelings and preserve our state of loneliness. We were taught that this was promoting holiness.

Fortunately, this young woman had both charm and sense, and, realising what was going on, courageously came to see me and asked if we could talk. She had an idea what was happening, and told me that she sensed I was attracted to her and that she was also attracted to me.

She said: 'If you ever decide to leave the priesthood, I would be very glad to develop a different relationship with you. However, if you remain a priest, and I think that you will, then you need not fear me. I will always respect your position as a priest, so why can we not remain friends?'

As a young priest that was a great liberating moment for me. While we were attracted to one another, there was no reason to avoid each other, provided we both respected the boundaries and commitments. We have remained friends, though we have both moved countries since that time.

I realise now that such friendships, and all the other friendships that help to weave our lives, are what allow us to grow as human beings. We avoid and neglect these at our peril, whether we are single, celibate, or married. Whether we are priests or lay people, married or single, we all have a deep longing for the infinite and all-liberating love.

While, as they say in AA circles, 'there is a heart-shaped hole at the centre of our being that only God can fill', human companionship is very important if we are to find maturity and, indeed, meaning in our lives.

Tom Winning

In 1968, I was appointed as assistant priest to Fr Thomas Winning, DD, who was parish priest at St Luke's, in Motherwell, a borough district of four parishes next to Hamilton. It was also part of the Clyde Valley industrial belt, which was famous for its steelworks and coal mines.

St Luke's was the smallest and poorest of the parishes. In truth, it required only one priest even then. Fr Tom worked every weekday at the Marriage Tribunal and Diocesan Office near Motherwell Cathedral, so this necessitated another priest to be available in the parish.

Tom was a great priest, with compassion for the sick and the needy. I recall attending a meeting at the office of the Provost, which was the equivalent of a mayor or town clerk, regarding the inordinate numbers of tenants being rehoused in St Luke's Parish because they did not pay the rent elsewhere in the borough. Tom argued powerfully, not only for the poor but also for the rights of the rent-paying citizens, who were being unfairly treated too, as a disproportionate number of unruly youths were being threatened by the Borough authorities that they would be dumped down to Forgewood, in St Luke's district, if they did not behave.

Another memorable event that took place in St Luke's was the formation of a Parish Pastoral Council in 1970. In this, Tom Winning was ahead of his time. He got a Dublin lady, who was a qualified statistician, to conduct a survey of all parishioners over sixteen years of age. They were asked for their response to existing lay groups within the parish and about what other works, sodalities, groups, or movements they would be interested in forming, or being part of.

The result was an elected Parish Pastoral Council of some ten groups, and two representatives elected from each street or area. It enabled various groups to form liturgies for week nights and, in general, gave people a sense of unity and a platform to be represented on.

However, in 1970 Tom was moved away to become Auxiliary Bishop in Glasgow. He suggested to me that I would be moved when the new man came in a few months and that I should consider further studies, having got a few months' notice of a pending move. I applied for a one-year diploma course in teacher training at the Vincentian College in Strawberry Hill, London, where I qualified in Religious Education and took Physical Education as a second subject.

As it turned out, the new parish priest at St Luke's had little or no enthusiasm for the Parish Pastoral Council and it ceased to function. The lesson for me was to question, yet again, a system of governance where one person could hold such power. For those of us not called, or indeed suited, to be a cardinal or bishop, it was disheartening to see years of work going down the tubes due to a system where one cleric decides not to call a meeting of the parish council.

This experience, and one or two others when I returned to Ireland, led me to consider another way of pastoral care for God's people, and to consider forming a basic Christian community.

Workaholism

On my return from Strawberry Hill Training College, I went on to teach religion in St Margaret's High School, Airdrie, in 1972. Looking back on that period, I have to admit that I made the mistake of working too hard, and of trying to do more than I was asked to do.

Bishop Thomson had asked me to be chaplain at the High School. However, when the headmaster heard that I was a qualified teacher he pleaded with me to take a full-time post at the school and set up a department of religion, so that the pupils would have a religious education class once a week. It seemed a good idea at the time and some great things happened, such as a fantastic production of *Jesus Christ Super Star* which began in that classroom. However, a couple of challenging things happened also.

Back home in Derry, tensions were mounting. On 30 January 1972 twenty-six civil rights protesters and bystanders were shot by British paratroopers in what became known as Bloody Sunday. Six of my brothers had been on the march that day, and they all gave me their reports of watching innocent people being shot down, with thirteen of them shot dead.

Deep down, memories of past injustices surfaced. I felt passionately for my people at home but did not know what I could do to help. I felt that the Church was standing back and doing nothing. I spoke with Bishop Winning and Bishop Thomson about the situation, and they were inclined to leave comments to the Irish church leaders, even though a large number of Scottish troops were involved in service in Ireland.

In those days, the Catholic Church in Scotland seemed very aware of being an immigrant church of a few generations, and was reluctant to rock the boat, or to challenge the policy of government in Northern Ireland.

Listening to the comments of the soldiers at Aldershot following Bloody Sunday, and watching a mid-week interview with those soldiers on Scottish television, it was clear that many of them had Scottish accents. One of the staff at the school where I taught was an ex-paratrooper, and did not take kindly to my comments after Bloody Sunday.

During a religious lesson with a senior class in St Margaret's High School, I explained to the pupils exactly why the people were marching that day. When they saw graphically on the black board that a small fraction of unionists controlled the larger population of nationalists, by a system of voting known as gerrymandering, the students agreed that the march was justified.

Around that time, to get me out of the teaching situation, Bishop Thomson appointed me chaplain to another smaller secondary school, and as curate to John Bosco Parish, in New Stevenson, where I was to work with a great priest called Fr Tom Barry. He had a lovely, kind personality. As I was sick with ulcers, it turned out to be the ideal place, and company, at that time.

On reflection, I made a mistake in taking up the teaching situation full-time without talking to Bishop Thomson. Call it the enthusiasm of youth. As a teacher himself, Bishop Thomson knew the benefits of a chaplain who was available to pupils and teachers, and was not identified too closely with the regime in the school, by being seen as just another religious teacher.

I apologised to him for what happened and we became good friends. He rang me quite often after that to talk about the ongoing troubles in Northern Ireland. He, like many of the clergy from East Scotland, knew little or nothing about the cause of the Troubles, the need for civil rights, and the gerrymandering, with its effects on housing allocation and job opportunities. However, via television news and newspapers, people in Britain and elsewhere became informed. Sadly, they were informed about the discrimination against the background of riots and deaths on the streets.

It would have been better for all of us if civilised society in Britain had become aware of the gerrymandering, and discrimination in housing and job allocations, and had acted to challenge the situation before violence broke out.

Charismatic Renewal

In those days, many of my friends were leaving the priesthood for various reasons, and I began to agonise over whether I should stay or not. The charismatic movement was a lifesaver for me at this time.

We had a study group in those early days. It was a group of about nine at most, made up of young priests who would study the documents of the Vatican Council and share together on a Friday afternoon. We became know as the Clonmacnoise group. We used to meet in Bailiston, at the home of Fr John Cosgrove, who was appointed chaplain to a nearby convent in his final years of ministry.

Despite the comradeship and mutual support, members of the group started dwindling and leaving the priesthood. One of them, Fr Mickey, showed me a notebook containing a list of names of the first group, and both of us remarked on the number that had left. I then learned the following week that the reason Fr Mickey had discovered that notebook was because he was packing up to leave as well!

It has always amazed me how we priests play our cards so close to our chests. Maybe it is the effect of the confidentiality associated with confessions, or good counsel, but we seem to find it hard to confide in others, even in one another, in matters that are personal. Perhaps the compulsory celibacy rule has something to do with it also. We get used to not expressing feelings of intimacy with a loved one, so it becomes par for the course not to talk about our feelings and struggles, in areas other than sexuality as well. At least, that is my impression.

I experienced Charismatic Renewal for the first time in 1973, when I met a Presbyterian elder in the local Church of Scotland, a lady, who gave me a book called *Nine o'clock in the Morning*, by Dennis Bennett. In it I read about forgiveness, about the reality of the power of Jesus Christ, about the Lord being alive in our hearts, and about the power of the Holy Spirit and His gifts that enable us to prophesy, to teach, and to pray for healing in a faith-filled way.

I had heard about these things before, but here, for the first time, I was reading about somebody who had actually experienced the reality of them, and I was very excited about that. I remember reading it and thinking that this is the way I had always thought it could be, and should be. Somehow, God needs to be experienced as real if we are to become enthusiastic Christians.

I read the book sitting in the chapel, and I had a sense that this was the start of a new era. It engendered a new hope in me. It was like coming alive again; being renewed in my spirit. I became more at peace with myself and with others. Around that time, I felt that the prayer we said for a new Pentecost, when we were praying for the outcome of the Second Vatican Council, was being answered. Certainly, the documents we reflected on at our Friday meeting, and at Deanery meetings in the diocese, seemed to become more relevant.

The same was also true of the Bible. The Word of God was beginning to become a living word for today. Later, I told my bishop that I now felt called to go back to work in Ireland for reconciliation, as we could see from news reports and communication with people at home, that the situation was not improving. Bishop Thomson listened and asked me to pray and reflect more on this. This discernment process went on for another year.

Around the same time as my move to be with Fr Tom Barry, my old priest friend, Fr John Cosgrove rang and asked if I would go to a prayer meeting in the house of a friend of his up in Sterling. He needed me to drive him, so, as a courtesy to him, I went.

I was feeling a bit deflated at the time as I had been changed from one parish to another, and changed out of a school. Looking back now, it was the only time in my life when I can recall being a bit depressed, though I did not know it then. I was not sleeping well, and was going out at nights on my own for long walks. I was unable to express my feelings and so did not seek company. Those who know me now would find this difficult to believe. I suspect that period was a preparation time for the years since then, when I was to pray with many oppressed, and depressed, people.

Fr Cosgrove's friend, a recovering alcoholic, had a fourteen-year-old daughter who was suffering from leukaemia. There were just the four of us at the prayer meeting: an old retired priest, a recovering alcoholic, a girl with leukemia and a depressed curate. Quite a set up!

As we sat around a table with a lighted candle and a Bible on it, song sheets were passed around, and the other three started singing. As they reverently sang the hymn 'Spirit of the living God fall afresh on me', which I heard sung for the first time that day, I began to get an inner peace.

I found myself sitting there smiling and thinking how I had not smiled for months. I was experiencing the anointing and blessing of God, and it was the beginning of something new. The Holy Spirit, like the wind, blows where He wills. Since that, I have often sensed the power of the Spirit, but that day stands out in my memory as a special day of blessing.

As the Troubles progressed in Ireland, I was fortunately in a very peaceful environment, and with a great youth group in the parish of St John Bosco. Time for prayer returned into my life and time also to have a day off, playing golf with my priest friends, Alo Cunnane, Brian Logue and, for a time, Fr Kevin O'Doherty.

That period at John Bosco's, between 1972 and 1975, was a great time in my life. The work in the parish, in the local secondary school, and with the thriving youth club, was complemented by studying at night for a sociology degree via the Open University.

Over the three years that followed, I often spoke with Bishop Thomson about my sense of having something to give back at home. It was against that background that I got his permission to write to the Bishop of Derry and seek an appointment as a priest to work in the Derry Diocese.

I sensed I had a calling to promote reconciliation in my home diocese, where people were suffering from the effects of the Troubles. The decision to come home came from a desire to make a difference. It was a major step, and one that would lead me into good times as well as into very stressful and painful times.

Ministering in Derry

To my searching mind, the answer to the Troubles lay in the work of reconciliation, and in preaching and teaching about Christ as the only one who could overcome the evil of violence, both physical and institutional.

In 1975 I was given an appointment to serve as curate in St Eugene's Cathedral, in Derry. I was chaplain to St Joseph's Secondary School and, along with the ordinary duties of a curate, I founded the St Joseph's Charismatic Prayer Group, through which I encouraged lay ministry, teaching, prayer for healing and counselling. These were much needed in the Derry of the mid-seventies, when the Troubles were at their height.

Derry today, now a celebrated City of Culture, has certainly moved on from the Derry of the mid-seventies. Then, we had almost daily bombings, shooting incidents, riots, army raids, deaths and grief in plenty. I recall some horrific stories.

During my first month there, I was preparing for a final examination in a Sociology degree which I had begun in Scotland. It was a warm day, and the window was open in my room, in the parochial house of the cathedral, which overlooked the traffic lights at the corner of Creggan Road and Windsor Terrace. Suddenly, loud machine gunfire rang out killing two policemen in plain clothes, who were coming from the Creggan police station just up the road. After the fright, I looked out to see their car slowly drift off and crash into the pillar nearby, with their two dead bodies left inside.

An old woman, who had witnessed this after coming from the corner shop, told me that she was approached by one of the gun men afterwards who comforted her with the words: 'It's ok dear. It's all over now.'

A short time later, I had the difficult task of having to tell a woman on that very street that her husband had been shot dead in another attack outside the city. He was approached by a man in the bar he was in, who asked him if his name was John Toland. John was a barman and was shot dead simply because he was a Catholic. The killer was eventually caught and tried but got off on a technicality.

I went on my knees beside his wife, Marie, as the children gathered round very soon after the shooting. We prayed, as there was little else that was going to bring any consolation. Only recently I was speaking with some of those children, now grown adults. They got the grace not to harbour any bitterness towards their father's killer.

In those days I smoked the pipe. I would listen to people in the parish waiting room for ages while smoking the pipe. When someone did that it appeared to people that they had the answer to the problem, but were just not giving it yet. In that sense, it became a smokescreen in more ways than one! However, after a year or so, on attending a prayer for healing at a prayer meeting, I got to forget about the pipe, thank God.

Gradually, I realised that people with problems did not need good advice, but more often required prayer, either silent or audible.

When someone came in pain or grief following a death, or to talk about their son who was recently 'lifted' and imprisoned, there was very little we could do as clergy. I became more aware that prayer would bring consolation and courage to those stricken souls.

We would telephone the police contacts that we had in order to get the story, and would be told where the person in captivity was being held, and when the relative could come and visit. But the big help that we were all thrown back on was prayer.

For the first six months or so, we held the prayer meetings in the Northlands Rehabilitation Centre for alcoholics and drug addicts. I was astounded at the power of God released in those gatherings; people were healed in mind and body, miraculous things happened in abundance.

Later, we held the weekly meeting in St Joseph's School, Creggan, where around two hundred would assemble. Ted Armstrong, the headmaster, became a very enthusiastic attendee. Indeed, so enthusiastic did he become that he changed his punishment method for students from strapping them to giving them long Bible passages to read and learn. To this day, Ted is a great supporter of Columba House, and was an active member of the Columba Community for years.

As a result of these prayer meetings, I felt a need to go to the roots of where Charismatic Renewal started. While it had its beginnings in Duquesne, in Pennsylvania, America, I went to Ann Arbour, Michigan, where there was a big community at the time founded by Ralph Martin, who would be the best known of the lay leaders of the Charismatic Movement in the Catholic Church. Ralph Martin went on to be appointed by Pope Benedict XVI, in December 2011, as a consulter to the Pontifical Council for Promoting the New Evangelisation, much required in the Catholic Church today.

I went with my old priest friend, Fr Cosgrove, to the United States in 1976 for my annual holidays, and I remember saying when I came back from there to St Eugene's that the experience was like being ordained all over again.

We had been in America for a month, visiting charismatic renewal centres and attending conferences, including a conference at Steubenville College, Ohio, attended by four hundred priests. Tremendous things happened at that conference, and, I suppose, that is where I began to really appreciate charismatic renewal, and the central place the movement had for renewing the Church, if the Church people would say 'yes' to what was on offer.

I was so tired, at one point, listening to talk after talk in a big marquee that I went out to lie in the sun for a while. Fr Francis Martin, an eminent Scripture scholar who was a lecturer in Washington DC at the time, was giving a talk on 'The Normal Christian Life'.

Fr Francis spoke about the four pillars of normal Christian life as he saw it. He spoke about prayer, Christian community, evangelisation, and reconciliation as the four pillars of the normal Christian life.

After his initial remarks about the centrality of prayer in the Christian life, Fr Martin went on to speak about building Christian community. He defined Christian community as 'a network of interpersonal relationships, based on our individual relationship with Jesus Christ as the cornerstone; the Saviour'.

He then spoke about evangelisation before finishing with the crucial topics of reconciliation and repentance. He believed that these four concepts contained all that was needed to lead a happy, holy and fulfilled life as a Christian. This had a profound effect on me.

Confirmation on the journey

When I returned from this inspiring conference I was plagued with doubts about the reality of my experience, and was being tempted to set it all aside as a passing whim.

With my sister Angela, *c.*1959.

My parents at the ancient monastic ruins at Enagh Lough, Strathfoyle, Co. Derry.

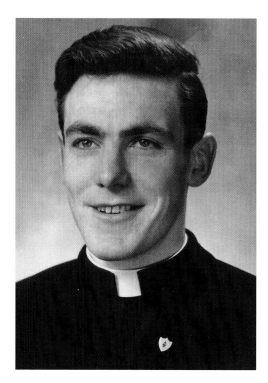

Ordination day at St Peter's,
Wexford, 1964.

My mother, May,
pictured in May 1989.

With my family at a gathering to celebrate
my 25th anniversary as a priest, 1989.

Having won the mile race and a
few other events I received the
Victor Ludorum 'winner of the
games', St Peter's, Wexford, 1960.

A gathering of the Columba Community on the day I won my first Clerical Golf Tournament in the mid-eighties.

The core members of the St Joseph's Charismatic Prayer Group, taken at a farewell meal we shared together before I went back to Scotland in 1979. Included are Columba Community members, Tommy and Ann McCay.

Revd David Armstrong, Limavady, and Billy McIlwaine, a preacher from Shankill Road in Belfast, during a Mass of Reconciliation celebrated on the lawn of my home in Ludden, Fahan, in Co. Donegal around 1979, during the early days of the Columba Community.

Early days at Columba House, Queen Street, Derry, 1980. With, front l–r: Margaret Fagan, Sam McColgan, Tommy and Ann McCay, and, back l–r: Tommy Cassidy, Brian Doherty, Billy Doherty, Sean Boyle and Michael McKinney.

In 2002 with Fr Jim Burke, a Dominican priest from Chicago, who visited Columba House annually for almost thirty years. We first met at a conference in Ireland in 1977. Jim was an inspiration to me and a great blessing to the Columba Community, in guiding us on how to wait on the Lord's guidance and how to build a Christian community.

Cardinal Tom Winning with me at
Columba House on 9 June 1997, for the
celebration of St Columba's Feast Day.

Columba's Day outside the Guildhall in Derry, 9 June 1985.

Paschal Fires Throughout Ireland
Easter 1988

A sketch map of the Paschal fires that were lit around Ireland on Holy Saturday night in 1988. Fires were also lit at various locations in England as a symbol of the Light of Christ being illuminated.

1. SLANE
2. SCALP
3. FAHAN
4. NEWRY
5. CORRYMEELA
6. BALLYSHANNON
7. CLONFERT
8. LISDOONVARNA
9. CORK
10. DUBLIN
11. ATHLONE
12. BELFAST
13. CARNDONAGH
14. CLONMANY
15. CELBRIDGE
16. ARAN ISLAND
17. CLAREMORRIS
18. BUNCRANA
19. GREYSTEEL
20. TWINBROOK
21. TRIM
22. SLEMISH
23. CLAREMORRIS
24. SALTHILL
25. DOWNPATRICK
26. MALIN
27. MAGHERA
28. SLIGO
29. BELFAST
30. MULLINGAR
31. ENNISCORTHY
32. FOXFORD
33. BALLYOWEN
34. BALLYBRACKEN

Bishop Seamus Hegarty with Fr Neal Carlin, his mother, May, and other members of the Columba Community at Columba House, following their inauguration as a lay institution during a ceremony of recognition in St Eugene's Cathedral in 1995.

I was reflecting on this in my sitting room in St Eugene's parochial house one afternoon. There and then, I knelt down, and was imploring God's guidance when a really powerful thing happened.

The intercom telephone in my room rang. As I got up to answer it, the knowledge came to me that there would be a middle-aged woman in the office, who had two teenage children, was separated from her husband, and wished to go to Confession. When I lifted the telephone all that the housekeeper, Mary McDaid, said was: 'There is a woman in the office who wants to see a priest.'

As I went down three flights of stairs I thought, if this knowledge I have about this lady is accurate then I will believe Jesus lives, and 'speaks to men's hearts'. After hearing her confession, I asked her why she had come just now to Confession. I was not really surprised when she revealed that the circumstances of her life were exactly as I had been told by the Lord in my heart. She had been passing in a taxi that day when something almost compelled her to get out and visit the cathedral, and, after a while praying, she found she wanted to go to Confession.

Little did she know how the Lord had used her to convince me to take His Word seriously, and to begin to listen, and trust. I thanked her for coming. Since that initial lesson, both in my own life and in the lives of my praying companions, I have, generally speaking, known God's direction and will. The joy and peace of following His promptings abide in times of trial and suffering.

Over the next two years I saw the love, and power, of God to heal and comfort, and bring great joy and peace to many people. The St Joseph's Prayer Group grew to three hundred people of expectant faith, who praised God with a new awareness, and became baptised in His Holy Spirit.

I was attending prayer meetings, praying with people day in

and day out, hearing Confessions like never before, and people were coming to me with problems that they never would have expressed before. There was a current of expectation.

A big international charismatic conference was held in Ballsbridge, Dublin, in 1978, and I decided to invite Frs Francis McNutt, Francis Martin, John Bertolucci and Michael Scanlan, who was the president of the Charismatic Renewal Committee in America, to Derry. They were all international speakers who had been visiting Dublin and holidaying in Donegal.

They were very enthused by the spiritual renewal, and I brought them up to meet Bishop Edward Daly. I got a word from the Spirit that day as I came down the bishop's stairs. It stated: 'Your head is going to roll.' A couple of weeks later, I received a letter from Bishop Thomson saying that there had been a request for me to be recalled to Scotland.

The day I received that letter, Bishop Daly came into the dining room at lunchtime and asked me to come to see him. He asked if I had received a letter from my bishop. I said that I had, and he asked me how I felt about this. I told him that I was totally shocked, and he then told me that I was welcome to stay on for another year. I asked him, if all went well during that year, would I be welcome to stay for good, as that was what was originally agreed to happen after the first two years. But he said that it would just be one year and that would be it.

I recall stating that I would need to go and speak with Bishop Thomson, as he would be wondering what was going on, and Bishop Daly told me to take whatever time I needed to see my bishop.

On leaving the cathedral a few days later, I went home to my parents in Fahan. When I told them the situation, my father said: 'I told you years ago not to trust those men!' He meant bishops, and he had told me that exactly twenty years earlier, when I announced at eighteen years of age that I was going to the seminary to study to be a priest. He had been disappointed, as he had wanted me to help out in the family business.

To this day, I don't really know why I was not able to continue my ministry in Derry. That was a very painful time. I had considered myself married to the Church, but at this point I felt betrayed. I actually experienced a physical pain in my stomach which went through to my back. I recall telling this story to a counsellor in the monastery of Pecos, when I went on a six months' sabbatical to reflect and pray, and he told me to spend time getting in touch with the pain, and that the forgiveness would come later.

In time, the Lord healed me, but it took a long time. The letting go of resentments is the secret and that requires God's special grace. We need to beg God for the gift of being able to say with Jesus on the cross, 'Father forgive them. They know not what they do.'

Years later, I was praying for a way of letting go, once and for all, of this recurring memory of hurt. I needed to really let go. This is what happened. I saw myself in a prison cell, and Jesus was standing in the corridor on the other side of the prison bars. He looked like the stereotype figure we have been presented with, yet very ordinary and humble. He had a key, and asked me did I want out of prison. I said that I did.

Then Jesus showed me the key, but before He gave it to me He asked if I knew who was in the next cell, and in the cell next to that. The correct answer dawned on me. I said that I did. They were the two people I had had difficulty with during my time in St Eugene's Cathedral, and that I had felt hurt by. There was a third cell, and the person in it was dressed in white. I wondered if that was someone I had hurt, or just another innocent victim. Maybe it was an image of Jesus himself, or an angel, I don't know.

The Lord told me that when I opened the door of my cell, it would open all the doors on that wing, or corridor. If I was to get out of there, then I also needed to be willing to let the others out, and to be reconciled with them. I agreed to do that. I opened the door, and went out.

Next, I saw myself warmly shaking hands with the first person, then the second and the third, and we all walked down the corridor together to the left. We came to a large steel door. The key, which had a handle as big as a chair seat, was in the door, and there was a huge long bar in the corner. It required four people to open the door. We had to put the bar into the key handle. Two of us pulled up, and two pushed down, to get the door open, and when it opened there was a beautiful light. It was just a silver and gold radiant vacuum. I think it was an image of Heaven. It was lovely, healing and peaceful.

We cannot get free or go to God's peace alone. We need to want that for all others as well. A lot of people do things, and do not ever think that they are hurting others. If we are able to willingly bless people who have hurt us, then our hearts will be free. All I know is that since that experience I have never looked back, or had any sense of resentment towards those in the vision.

I feel it is important for me to clearly state that I honestly believe that God was in all of this, and that I also required forgiveness for my faults. God has His unique ways of purifying us, and getting us better placed to do His will. I have always sensed that I was released for a reason, so, in a way, I owe a great debt of gratitude to those whose actions led to me having to leave the cathedral parish in Derry. May God continue to bless them here and hereafter.

The above experience was to culminate for me in what I had sensed the Holy Spirit was pushing me towards from the day I left the cathedral parish. Had I not been set aside in this way, the

Columba Community would never have been established in Derry. I did pray for a close-knit Christian community of prayer, who would listen and work together. So, be careful what you pray for, or at least be prepared to pay the price of an answered prayer.

Freedom to minister

The problems that priests faced in Derry City were certainly compounded by the era known as the Troubles. The riots by local youths, the shootings and bombings by the provisional Irish Republican Army, together with the raids by police and army, caused havoc, and immense stress on the population.

How normal life continued to happen is a testimony to the resilience of the people. Schools stayed open and other statutory bodies continued to serve the people, despite personal risk to life and limb. People simply got used to bombings and killings.

One of the memories I have that illustrates this is when my brother-in-law and I were stopped at lights on the main Strand Road, in the heart of the city. As we sat in the car, a bomb went off locally. Two women were looking in a shop window, and I noticed that neither of them even turned around, so familiar were they to the daily sound of bombs in the mid-seventies.

Having returned from Scotland, I was very aware of how the clergy were fulfilling roles that would be performed by police in any normal society. These included signing passports, and other official documents. Then again, this reliance on priests in Derry was something that had gone back a long time before the Troubles.

If I was questioning the system of governance when the pastoral council was dispensed with at the whim of a priest in Scotland, I certainly was confirmed in that questioning after my experience in Derry.

It is actually unfair on the bishop of a diocese to burden him with sole responsibility. The system breeds an unhealthy type of conformity, and a lack of divergent thinking. It certainly would not attract enthusiastic young men, who need support to live and give the Good News in today's society, where respect for difference and proper levels of shared responsibility is called for.

To push home this point, I recall a 'care for clergy' programme that was promoted in the Derry Diocese some years ago. A priest from the Westminster Diocese facilitated us to eventually develop support groups, walking groups, prayer, or study groups, etc. In preparation for these, an in-depth survey was conducted and the main findings were interesting, especially for the few of us who were divergent thinkers.

The facilitator stated that of all the dioceses he had ever helped with this programme, the Derry one was unique. It showed that larger numbers of clergy were very compliant, unquestioning, and submissive to authority. The facilitator then illustrated that while this predominant attitude may help in conformity, it was a characteristic that verged on blind, unquestioning obedience, and, on occasions, could be very unhealthy and contribute towards abuse of authority.

Given the exposure of this problem over recent years in the Church, surely we need to seek together how best to use positions of influence to serve and guide, rather than to drive through in a heavy-handed way. The survey helped me to realise that we clergy help create the type of authority that we have.

When I was a student living at Fahan, our local parish priest, a humble and learned gentleman, had to go to meet his bishop back in the early sixties. The little priest was suffering from chronic ill health. He was absolutely terrified at the prospect of the visit. As a young student, I remember thinking how sad and pitiful the scene was.

We are all responsible for the kind of climate and culture we develop. I wondered if the effect of this particular bishop on the clergy was still evident in that survey of clergy attitudes in Derry. A culture of fear and, therefore, lack of honest dialogue had developed between clergy and bishop, which transferred itself also to the people–clergy relationship. To acknowledge that is to begin to change, so that the frustration that has produced anger may give way to respectful conversation, where we search together for better, and more Christian, relationships.

One of the things that enabled me to decide to continue as a Catholic priest, working alongside, and eventually within, the diocesan system, was my experience of communities where levels of lay participation in decision making and active ministry were witnessed.

This gave me hope of new ways of empowering the laity, implementing new governance systems, and, in particular, developing lively, faith-filled communities where we can use the gifts of the Holy Spirit. This is not so new, when we read about the early church in the Acts of the Apostles and the Church fathers, together with what we know about the Celtic monastic Church.

To this end, some of us have been developing the Columba Community over the past thirty-five years. This has involved the cross and experience of weakness and limitations. It requires that we forsake the over-reliance on our own intellect, and seek again the mind and ways of God, who often chooses to build His Kingdom on our weaknesses.

Maybe brought low, and to our knees, as a church in Ireland can be the very opportunity for a new beginning, and the new Evangelisation Pope John Paul II and his successors called for.

Christian leaders are called to be led by Christ's ideas, not their own ideas. The 'business as usual' type church has not worked.

The new way of evangelising needs to be promoting Jesus Christ in a way that hungry souls may begin to know Him as loving Saviour and Lord in their lives. He is the only rock on which to rebuild the church, and yet Catholics, for some reason, do not hear this message clearly.

I finish this chapter with a quote from the book *Jesus of Nazareth*, by Gerhard Lohfink: 'God's realm can happen only when human beings collide with their own limits, where they do not know how to go on, where they hand themselves over and give space to God alone so that God can act. Only there, in the zone of constant dying and rising, the reign of God begins.'

The visible sign of this unimaginable reign of God, however, is the people of God, or the church.

Columba House of Prayer and Reconciliation

On my return to Scotland in late autumn of 1978, I went on retreat to pray about what was happening in my life. I then took a six-month sabbatical, which I spent in the United States visiting some basic Christian communities.

When I returned, I spoke with Bishop Thomson, and he permitted me to stay in Ireland for a period while I tried to discern properly where the Lord was leading me. I felt very strongly that I was meant to work in Ireland. It would have been easier to return to Scotland where I was always welcome, but that did not seem to be the call of God in my life.

So, in June 1979, I came back to Ireland, where Cardinal O'Fiaich was exceptionally supportive of my position. I started work as a kind of freelance chaplain in the prisons, and I used this time to wait, as I felt instructed to by the Lord, to see what was going to happen in my life next.

During this time of waiting, I felt encouraged by the Cardinal's genuine openness, friendship and understanding, which I wrote about in an edition of *An Creggan*, a periodical published in Armagh, with which he was associated until his untimely death. I cannot overstate my admiration for him.

On occasions when I felt tired, and somewhat alone, or disillusioned, with the system, I was welcomed by Cardinal O'Fiaich to join him for lunch and a chat. This would generally happen on a Sunday on my return from offering a couple of Masses at Long Kesh prison. He was always interested in the well-being of prisoners of all kinds, and, indeed, welcomed a loyalist friend of mine, who had changed his ways of thinking.

Around that time, Cardinal O'Fiaich was severely criticised by the southern national papers. He was misunderstood by a media that did not seem to know the difference between an outspoken, knowledgeable, and truthful nationalist, and an avid, active republican. They, like some people I met in America, thought it was a religious war. Sadly, what added to their confusion and misconception was the religious fundamentalism and belief that home rule was Rome rule, which prevailed among loyalists.

Shortly before the Cardinal died I had lunch with him. On a previous visit, I had mistakenly taken a fountain pen, an ink-filled Parker, which I then mislaid. I bought a replacement, and when I offered it to him he thanked me, saying: 'I will remember you, Niall when I use this.' Sadly enough, the last writing he did with that Parker pen was to sign himself into the hospital that he was flown to from Lourdes.

On leaving his house for what turned out to be the last time, I recall asking for his blessing. After praying a lovely blessing, he then knelt down in his hallway and asked for my blessing. I remember him saying: 'Niall, give me your blessing. We met first just after I got the red hat, now I feel we are at the end of an era.'

I wonder did he have a premonition, or some indication, of the fact that his time on earth would be short. We often hear of such things. I was aware of the privilege of praying with a cardinal in Ireland, and, at the same time, not having a bishop or diocese in Ireland in which to be recognised. God's ways are strange.

Small steps were taken to form a praying community in Derry. I gave retreats to charismatic renewal groups all over Ireland, worked in a youth workshop one day a week, and in an alcoholic rehabilitation centre in Derry for a day each week as well.

One priest, Fr Seamus O'Connell, invited me to celebrate Sunday Mass and preach in his parish in Carnhill. I will always appreciate that gesture, and we have remained close friends. Fr Seamus was very much led by the Holy Spirit in his ministry too, and I recall praying and talking with him late into the night, back in 1976, about the things I had experienced.

Another priest who always made me welcome was Fr Michael Collins, who was the parish priest at St Columba's, Long Tower. These friendships were a great comfort in those early days, and helped in ways that are difficult to describe.

After a long wait, and much prayer, the answer I was waiting for came. It was in the spring of 1980, and I was sitting in Bethany House, in Wexford, praying and listening to the Lord, with a Church of Ireland Minister, Revd Norman Ruddock, his wife Jean and Fr Bob Staples, who had been my spiritual director in the seminary.

We had been praying in tongues, and afterwards there was a great silence, and a great sense of God's presence. Inwardly, I found myself crying out to God for Derry and its youth. Then I sensed the Spirit of the Lord directing me as follows: 'In a few days' time you will meet a stranger who will point out a house to you.'

That was an exciting time. The message was real, and very encouraging. I spoke to Norman and Jean about it on the way home, and I have often been grateful that I did, as, on reflection, it was proof that this really did happen and was not just my imagination.

A few days later, I was in the alcoholic rehabilitation centre in Derry when a man came up to me during coffee break and said: 'I believe you travel to prison each week and work with prisoners and their families. What you need is a large house and I know where you can get one.'

He brought me down to Queen Street to a bombed-out site, which had once been a house used by the police for lodging and recreation. I found this very symbolic; the Lord was using a former police house, bombed-out by the Provos, as a place of renewal and reconciliation.

The Lord shows himself in these little details, and this is what you discover when you are waiting, watching and listening. I think the Lord delights in saying, 'I wonder will he get this insight.'

I was looking at four storeys of rubble, and I just knew that this was it – the site for Columba House. I had two hundred pounds in my pocket, an old broken-down car, and no income. I did not know how it was going to come about, but I knew that it was right, and that it would happen.

One morning I woke up with the name of a local developer, Colm Duffy, on my mind, and I went to see him. Colm and I did athletics together many years before. He was a busy man, and I remember him saying: 'Neal, I don't have a lot of time, what is it?' I responded with two sentences: 'There is an old house in Queen Street. You buy it and I will live in it.'

He looked at me for about three seconds and said: 'That's ok. Where is it?' It was as simple as that. I told him it was number eleven, and he said that he knew of it as he already had his eye on it. He bought the building, and had it almost restored when he went bankrupt. He told me that he was going to have to sell the house in a couple of weeks to somebody who would give him a good price, unless I could come up with the money – thirty thousand pounds. The pressure was on.

Manna from Heaven

Lying awake one morning at six o'clock, I was thinking about what to do when the name of someone I had met six months previously, for about ten minutes during a retreat in Dublin, came to me. I somehow knew that if I drove to Dublin I would see him at seven o'clock that night. I felt '7 p.m.' was the time I was given.

I arrived at the house of a relative of mine around four o'clock, and I rang the man's office for an appointment. His secretary said that it was impossible as he had a lot of meetings, including one with his accountant, who was flying in from London.

I told her my contact telephone number and asked her to ring me, if she could, at around five o'clock, and let me know what was happening. When she responded that she had just told me what was happening, I told her that I had a great certainty that I would be meeting with him at seven o'clock.

She rang me back at five o'clock to say that she did not know what had happened, but the meeting with the accountant and another meeting had been cancelled, and that I was welcome to meet the businessman for dinner at seven o'clock in his penthouse suite, at a hotel in the centre of Dublin.

I met him as planned, and a couple of hours later I walked out of the place with ten thousand Irish pounds. I remember thinking to myself on the way home that I was either the greatest conman alive or the Holy Spirit was at work. I knew the latter had to be true, as the guy was a shrewd businessman yet he handed me ten thousand pounds with no strings attached! The rest of the money came in just as dramatically.

We needed another twenty thousand, and we had a deadline. At that time, I had been asked to say the noon Mass and preach at Carnhill. It was during the summer of the first Hunger Strike. At the Mass was a local accountant, John Bradley, with his family, and he wrote to me afterwards regarding my sermon.

Apparently, I had spoken about the way forward being one of healing, forgiveness, and attempts at reconciliation, and also told some good news about prisoners who had come to see the futility of further violence, and now worked and prayed for peace.

In his letter, he offered me his support for the work of reconciliation. When I explained about the finance, he arranged with his bank manager to give us a loan. John then arrived one morning when we were at Morning Prayer and apologised, as his bank manager had contacted him at home the night before to say that he had been speaking with a senior cleric in the diocese regarding the proposed loan to me, and towards Columba House. As a result the deal was called off. The power of 'parish pump politics' is what my dad would have called that. Imagine, amid the Troubles of Derry in 1981, this was happening.

John wondered why I did not seem annoyed. In fact, if the truth were told, I felt happy. I recall telling him not to worry as I felt that we should never owe the banks money anyway, and that we would get an interest-free loan, or get a donation.

I later wrote in my first small book, *Freedom to Captives* about the injustices of banks. This was back in 1983. I had read two articles on the same page of a newspaper. One was about a man who had drowned in the River Thames in London because he owed a bank a couple of thousand pounds, and the other was about the millions of pounds' profit for that year that the same bank had made. I quoted the case of Anthony of Padua, in the eleven hundreds, persuading the city fathers, the bankers of the day, to decrease the interest rate they had imposed on the poor. I wondered whatever had happened to the sin of usury we had learned about in the seminary. That referred to the sin of extorting an unfair interest rate from a loan, and was based on biblical directives on justice. Did we, as a church, become too much part of the problem?

God answers prayer
By this stage, members of the evolving Columba Community were meeting for early Morning Prayer at seven o'clock in one of the completed rooms in the house at Queen Street, while others came along later for prayer, and to do some voluntary work, such as plastering, painting and tidying up.

One day, while I was praying in the oratory within the house, an old colleague of mine from Letterkenny, Owen Corrigan, a retired psychiatrist, came to visit, and during a conversation with one of the volunteers working on the bottom floor it was mentioned that we were twenty thousand pounds in debt. In fact, while we have never been in debt to the bank, we needed some thirty thousand pounds to purchase the premises.

Owen, whom I had met during a retreat I was giving for nurses and medical people in Ards Retreat Centre, in Co. Donegal, later came to me and asked if I would be embarrassed if he gave me twenty thousand pounds free of interest for as long as I needed it. I brought him over to my accountant, John Bradley, who often tells the story of this joyful answer to prayer when he speaks about the beginnings of Columba House.

Apparently, the generous doctor had recently received a large sum on his retirement. He had prayed about what to do with it, and felt that the Lord wanted him to use it for some good purpose. So, he put his retirement cheque in an envelope, placed it on top of his wardrobe, and waited. Then he came to visit me, as he had sensed that the Lord wanted me to have a loan of it.

That is how the Lord provided for the building of what became Columba House, a centre for prayer and reconciliation. So, I do not have to be told that the Lord is good, and that He will stick by you if you stick by Him. Indeed, it is my experience that when the Lord speaks to hearts, many strange and beautiful things happen.

The donor got his £20,000 back in four years, five thousand each year. He told me later that his bank manager had calculated that by his generous deed he, in fact, had made more interest than he would have had he put this money in the bank. Apparently, the fluctuation of the exchange between the punt and the pound those days yielded him some interest, while we paid back only what we had received. There is a Scripture which says that God will not be outdone in generosity, and that has been proven true in many of the experiences we have had.

While we got help by relying on God's Providence, there were tough times as well, and times of temptation. Good works and new efforts to follow the Spirit of the Lord have always had opposition, and the building of Columba House of Prayer and Reconciliation was no exception.

I clearly recall being approached by a certain man who, a reliable source informed me, was an active member of a paramilitary group. He told me he could get all the money I needed, and that all I had to do was to say nothing about where it came from. Building a place to pray and work for reconciliation, needless to say, required that we be very clearly in nobody's pocket, so the offer was refused.

The local residents' committee from around Queen Street, led by a city councillor, opposed our work, stating that such a centre as that envisaged by us would 'lower the tone of the entire area'. They managed to stop our renovations, with the planning authorities stating that we were diverting from the original use of the rooms and building. That was not true, as we had kept all the rooms in the same shape as they had been prior to the bomb. The fact that this building had long since moved from being a family residence to being a place where the police, the Royal Ulster Constabulary, had been staying in large numbers, seemed to be news to the chief planning officer.

Some time later, I was asked by my good friend, Revd John Morrow to speak on our work in prisons to the Corrymeela Community in Co. Antrim. I spoke for a while about the good things that were happening, in that many were turning away from violence to seek justice by peaceful means, and then I spotted the chief planning officer in the audience and figured that he was a member of this community. I did not hesitate to express my amazement, and frustration, both with the planning authorities, who were holding up progress with Columba House renovations, and the misunderstanding that came from the unfounded fears expressed by the residents locally. Soon after that meeting, planning permission was obtained.

I have found that when some people in positions of power realise that you are vulnerable, in not having the local official hierarchy behind you, they seem to think that you are fair game for exploitation. This experience, and similar ones, has often led me to reflect on the plight of the marginalised and poor, who are further exploited simply because they have no power base to appeal to. Again, I would add that if clergy, in particular, and middle-class Catholics, such as the ones we were dealing with above, are ever to get the principals of God's Kingdom enacted on earth, they need to reach out from their comfort zones and help the vulnerable.

I have to admit that I get a kick out of beating the odds, and beating the system, but that does not make me a rebel. It must always be remembered that as well as the guidance of the Holy Spirit, I also had permission to be where I was from my own official bishop in Motherwell. I returned there every so often to make sure that support continued, as I do not agree with any cleric 'doing his own thing', without reference to a higher human authority, however distant.

I always managed to obtain letters from Scotland describing me as 'a reputable priest of the Diocese of Motherwell', with permission to minister in Ireland, and that continued up to 1995, when I was officially incardinated into the Derry Diocese under the leadership of Bishop Seamus Hegarty.

The Columba Community was founded in 1980 by the small group of people who were meeting regularly to pray, and seek direction. It became obvious that there was a great need for a 'House of Reconciliation', and since opening Columba House, our first Centre of Prayer and Reconciliation, on 9 June 1981, the feast of St Columba, we have been blessed by God and His people.

The name Columba was an obvious one for us, as Columba was the founder of Doire Colmcille when he established his monastery in the wooded area in 557. He was also a great reconciler, as we know from his work at the Convention of Drumceatt. It was at Drumceatt, near Limavady, that Columba was crowned 'King of the Bards' by the songsters and musicians that he protected when most of the chieftains were intent on dissolving them, or gravely limiting their freedom.

We in the Columba Community commit ourselves to using our prayer, talents, and finance for the benefit of the community and the apostolate, and have grown over the years to now having five centres of ministry in the Derry–Donegal area.

In writing this book, I occasionally reviewed my notes taken in those days in order to recall the feelings, and mentality that prevailed. It is so easy to forget the pain, the self doubt, the sense of alienation from the establishment that went on. Easy, that is, from the present stand point of being fully recognised, and validated. Easy because the community has been, through God's grace, a success, and has helped thousands of people in one way or another to have happier lives.

The angel of comfort
We had an ecumenical service with Revd Cecil Kerr on 9 June 1981, to celebrate the opening of Columba House. A few days before that, some of us had gathered around a small table in a room above the kitchen, and there we offered our first Mass in Columba House.

I had a very powerful experience during that first Mass. There were about six of us, and we were sitting reflecting after Holy Communion when I became fearful at the thought that I was out on a limb. I knew that I was not the type to give up, and I also knew that it would be a long wait; the hierarchy in the church would be slow to change. So, I felt I was facing into a long time of waiting, and difficulty. Yet day by day the power of God was so very real, and that is what kept us going.

I looked down the dark tunnel of perhaps thirty years of struggle and thought, how long is this going to last? Then I got this vision of somebody coming. A man walked in the front door wearing a big, off-white garb, and holding a long staff, or stick. I sensed as he walked through the hall, and began to climb the stairs, that it was Columba. He was a strongly built man, but not very tall, and I could see his face clearly. He looked like a fifty-year-old man, with long, shoulder length, grey hair. His forehead was clear of hair, and his face was strong and rounded. He looked peaceful, and like someone who knew where he was going. His eyes were kind – almost smiling. He walked right up and around the small gathering to my left shoulder, and I had this sense of anointing. He did not say anything, but I could feel that as he stood there, staff in hand, that he was telling me to stay with it, that he was at my side.

That had a big impact on me. It was an immense experience of God's power at work. From feeling somewhat afraid and apprehensive about what difficult times lay ahead, I changed to being at peace, and assured that all would be well eventually.

This kind of experience may seem unusual for a secular priest. Yet, I have come to accept that the journey I was asked to undertake was different, so why would the help not be different also. God was not going to leave me out on a limb without some extra help. It seems to me that such aids, and graces, come when we are not running the church or, indeed, our own lives as a 'business as usual' project. God, indeed, hears the cry of the poor, especially when the poor have no other answer.

I seldom shared this happening except with good friends, and community members. It was a very personal affirmation, and when I related it some years later to Bishop Seamus Hegarty, now retired, he advised me to get my true story written down as he felt that it would be a great pity if stories such as this were lost.

I came to give Good News to the poor

When Jesus was accused of eating with tax collectors and sinners, as recorded in Matthew's Gospel, he said that he had not come to call the righteous, but sinners. In my life, I have prayed with prisoners and their families during the Troubles, and then with alcoholics and their families.

The principles learned in those early days, of learning to trust God and have faith in Him, were invaluable in helping those we prayed with through our experiences. These happenings may seem strange to many, yet I emphasise that for a secular priest to stand his ground and do as I felt led to do, it was essential that such assurances came. That sense that the Lord was with us, together with the prayers of the community and support of family and friends, made all the difference between persevering and quitting.

It was somehow more important to me that God would provide for the need in the ways that He did. The sense of being led by the Spirit would not have been quite as strong had the bank agreed to give the loan. No man or woman could have assured me of God's will being done at Columba House. Yet, God did assure us by this experience during the opening Mass, and by the other events that surrounded the entire work.

Columba House contains a beautiful Blessed Sacrament Chapel, where over a hundred people a day visit for quiet prayer, and peace. It also provides a counselling service, and is a base for the youth outreach project, YARD (Young Adults' Reality Dreams). Our other centres include White Oaks Rehabilitation Centre, which is a centre for the treatment of addictions to alcohol, drugs and gambling, at Derryvane, Muff, in Co. Donegal, and the neighbouring IOSAS Centre, Sanctuary and Celtic Garden.

This community has been a blessing to thousands of people, especially those badly affected by the Troubles, and by addiction. To give an example, during the writing of this book, I was contacted by an anxious father, who wanted accommodation for his son who had been threatened with being shot through his knees for drug dealing. I doubt I would have been of much practical help to him had I still been busy in the day-to-day life of the parish. As it was, we persuaded this young man to come in for treatment. To begin with, he came for the wrong reasons and was in denial, but, in time, his motivation changed and he got the help that he needed to get his life in order.

It is not easy to compare the security of the parish work in St Eugene's Cathedral, with its constraints, to the type of ministry I became involved in at Columba House. But there was a very distinct difference between the dynamics at work. There was certainly a way in which my gifts as a person, and as a priest, were made available to people. Yet, there was an accompanying vulnerability in the position as well.

The weakness of my position, in not being officially appointed by the local bishop, resulted in many of my priest colleagues stating that I would last only a few years at most. Given the sense of calling and guidance from the Lord, however, I knew that was not an inspired statement. When we prayed in the early days, there was the sense that God would always choose the weak to confound the strong.

There is something about vulnerability which allows God to have His way, and we need to always reflect on that. Much of what we get involved in can be our will, our ideas, our projects, not God's will, not His ideas or His projects. Yet, when we sense His ways, and follow His promptings, there comes energy, a sense of purpose, and fulfillment, which is so different from what happens when we follow our own ideas.

A Celtic Saint and Pastor

A letter written in appreciation of the late Cardinal Tomas O'Fiaich, which was included in a special edition of An Creggan *magazine that was published as a tribute to the Cardinal. Creggan is near Crossmaglen, Cardinal O'Fiaich's home place.*

Columba House,
11 Queen Street,
Derry.

7 June 1990

Dear Fr McLarnon,

Ever since watching Cardinal O'Fiaich's sister-in-law on TV, I've been thinking of writing to you. I have, like so many others, lost a personal friend in Cardinal Thomas.

My work and position over the past eleven years here ... have been a bit unusual. It's been a profitable, sometimes painful and lonely walk. It was in that sense of loneliness and seeking affirmation, guidance and some security, that I found myself visiting Cardinal Thomas over the years. Coming from Donegal and ordained in St Peter's, Wexford ... gave us some common ground, when I first met his Eminence in 1979.

The Cardinal knew I was being called to work for reconciliation and for prisoners and their families and, in negotiations with my own Bishop Thomson, Motherwell, was instrumental in giving me the space I needed to do this work.

Over the years, Thomas O'Fiaich encouraged me to keep going. He wrote us letters of support and sent the odd donation towards our work. My memory of visiting this great human Irish-type saint on Wednesday, 17 January, this year is vivid. Busy though he was, he found time to meet my friends, be they ministers, ex-UVF, friends from the Shankill area or Columba Community members.

One memory I would like to share with you was, after two hours of chat in January, when the Cardinal encouraged me to keep up the work, I knelt down, asking him for his blessing on leaving, as somehow I sensed we'd both completed an era. He then prayed a lovely blessing. Having finished, he then knelt down and said: 'Niall, give me your blessing. We met first just after I got the red hat, now I feel we are at the end of an era.' I felt very moved that such a man in his position had so much humility and ability to make one feel at ease. Like the time I went to see him and he answered in an off-white, open-necked shirt, apologising for the 'unofficial dress'. I told him that it made me feel at ease. I honestly suspect he did that to make me feel at home.

As I awoke this morning, I jotted down the few lines enclosed. I feel I've lost a soul-friend, an *'anam cara'*, one who knew about such communities springing up all over Ireland and Europe – small monasteries of clergy and lay-people, founded by courageous, learned men like himself – men who trusted in God and didn't spare themselves in spending their Celtic lives for the Kingdom.

I am so glad I visited the Cardinal this year and thanked him for being 'the kind of father-figure I needed to talk to every so often'. He was glad to be that much-needed type of shepherd in Ireland. When I expressed that I was operating out of Charismatic authority rather than out of legal rational authority that comes from appointment, he said: 'What do you think St Patrick worked out of, Niall?' This man was so secure and unthreatened by the works of the Holy Spirit in today's Church, largely because of his great magnanimity of heart, but also because of his great knowledge of the History of the Church and the Celtic Church in particular.

May God raise up more shepherds like Thomas O'Fiaich – a true Irishman – a European – above all, a Christian.

Formation of Community

The Columba Community was founded on the four pillars of normal Christian life – prayer, community, evangelisation and repentance – which the eminent Scripture scholar and lecturer, Fr Francis Martin had talked about during the Steubenville Priests' Conference in America in 1976.

I attended this conference during my summer holidays, while I was still ministering as a curate in St Eugene's Cathedral, Derry. I recall being very tired, as my old friend, Fr Cosgrove and I were on a trip around the charismatic centres that were emerging in America in those days, and we had travelled from Ann Arbour, Michigan, a day or two beforehand.

I was inspired by the simplicity and comprehensiveness of the event. It was a lovely sunny day, so I stretched out on the grass rather than sit in the large marquee in which the conference was being held.

As I lay there listening to Fr Martin, who spoke loud and clear, a very vivid image came to my mind. It was of a small, but powerful fire, which was pure white at the centre, then glowing gold and then red. It was built in the shape of a cone made up from about eight or nine logs, laid in perfect formation and all equally alight. It was an unbelievably strong image.

Fr Martin was talking about community when I had this vision, but it took me a long time to equate the two. When people come together in love, a flame of faith and love is lit that no one person is responsible for, just like the logs in the image, which were all burning equally. If you were to remove any one log the flame in it would die, and if you were to take the logs away, one at a time, and separate them from one another, the fire would die. The logs would not stay alight on their own. The extra ingredient we call the fire comes from the logs burning, yet the fire is more powerful than all of them together.

That is a very good image of a Christian community operating the way it ought to. The sum total of all of the parts, when together in proper relationship, is greater than the individual parts. Love makes the difference, as there God is.

This image burned into my mind in more ways than one, and I knew then it was a prophetic image that would remain with me in the future to help build a powerful, but small, basic Christian community. It spoke loudly of personal commitment to God and to other people, and it spoke powerfully about evangelisation being a flame of light to other people, when we live the way we are called to live in Christian community.

If we all share together our prayer life, talents, time, and some of our finances for the good of each other, and for the good of the apostolate of the group, then that is basic Christian Community in action. People need to feel that they are valued in their community.

Fr Martin defined community in the way we in the Columba Community have defined it ever since. It is 'a network of inter-personal relationships based on our common, but individual, relationships with Our Lord Jesus Christ'.

The image I received now appears as a great wall-hanging in the main prayer room where we celebrate our weekly healing Mass in Columba House.

While the Columba Community was officially recognised and declared a lay institute canonically by Bishop Seamus Hegarty, when he came to the Derry Diocese in 1995, the community of

Prayer and Reconciliation was founded in 1981, with its centre being Columba House.

Many good things happened following the canonical recognition, though we have been faithful to our original vision and mission statements.

Our vision is 'that all people may find freedom and dignity through Christ for the greater glory of God', and our mission is 'to joyfully come together as a group of individuals, believing in and celebrating the power of Jesus Christ, for mutual support and to minister to other people'.

Our original brochure, printed in 1981, still acts as our review document when we meet twice yearly to look at our commitments and listen to the Lord for continued guidance on these central aspects of what we refer to as the normal Christian life.

It reads: 'As well as daily community prayer, we intercede privately under the Lordship of Jesus in an attitude of reverence, openness and obedience to the Word of God; keeping in mind the words of Isaiah 40:31, 'They that wait upon the Lord shall renew their strength. They shall mount up with wings as eagles. They shall run and not grow weary, walk and not grow faint.'

As a group with common experience of being 'held captive' in prison cells or by the forces of anger, guilt, fear, and hatred, we have learned how to appreciate each other's weaknesses and needs, as well as helped to develop each other's talents and gifts. We see Christian Community as 'a network of interpersonal relationships based on our common relationship with Jesus Christ as Rock and Cornerstone'.

As we prayed and grew together, the Lord led us to evangelise, to be a small light of hope in a troubled area, a leaven locally, especially among those wounded by violence and counter-violence, and our outreach included retreats, teaching Christian truths to prisoners and ex-prisoners, and counselling those wounded by division in our land and church, particularly families of prisoners.'

As we became more aware of His Love, we daily became more aware of the need to turn towards Jesus, to change, to repent gladly. As wounded healers, we have sought to provide a place of refuge for the troubled and broken seeking freedom.

One of the aims of the Columba Community is to further reconciliation, which happens when we experience healing, love, mercy and forgiveness. We believe that only by love, forgiveness, and trust, can the fear, pain, and mistrust in our society be cast out and a new life experienced.

This, in real terms, involves repentance, coming from the Latin word *repensare*, meaning to think again. While this refers to thinking, repentance has to do with a change of heart as well. The Lord says: 'I will remove your heart of stone and give you a heart of flesh.' Such change is certainly a gift of God and often comes when we are touched by God's love in His Word or in other people.

The Lord does not desire this healing between family members only, but for nations also to be involved in reconciliation, in seeking justice and peace. He wants ongoing involvement, deep searching, and much more from us than platitudes and gestures during the church unity octave each year.

Confessions at the Guildhall
It was with this in mind that Revd David Armstrong, Revd Alan Harper, Revd Liz Hewitt and I formed the Christians Together Movement. The first of our monthly meetings took place in November 1984 and consisted of prayer, praise, scripture sharing, teaching, and small group discussions.

We are never going to lose by admitting to God how frail and sinful we are. Repentance is central to any healing of relations. In the community sense, it takes the bite out of the division, and an outstanding memory of this is the Guildhall, in Derry, in 1985, when we felt led to hold a very central service of repentance.

For a period of six weeks, the three traditions, what I would call the Celtic Irish, the Scots Irish, or the Ulster Scots as they call themselves now, and the anglicised established tradition in this country, met together for two or three hours every Friday on the run-up to Easter in 1985.

Then, on Good Friday, a representative of the three groupings expressed repentance on behalf of each 'tribe', with each confession immediately followed by an intercessory prayer by a member of the other two groups.

The first was entitled 'The Confession of the Protestant Community' and was read by a local Protestant, who stated: 'Heavenly Father, as a member of the Protestant community, I confess and ask forgiveness on behalf of many for the past and present sins of our community, especially for: The blasphemy of using your name in pursuit of political or military advantage; the misuse of the democratic process by gerrymandering and threatened use of force; perpetuating in religious bigotry by discrimination in jobs and housing; supporting in moral or practical ways the men of violence who have murdered in our name; the failure of our clergy and people to challenge injustice and bigotry; and a slavish devotion to past victories and an elitist attitude to our faith.

'On behalf of many Protestants, who would confess these sins, and many more, I ask forgiveness and make a commitment to work for the Glory of God through Christ our Lord.'

The second was entitled 'The Confession of the Gaelic Irish' and was read by a local Catholic, who stated: 'As a representative of the Gaelic Irish, I confess and ask forgiveness for: The centuries of unresolved anger which have produced atrocities both here in Ireland and England; for professing to follow Christ yet failing to really forgive our enemies; for glorifying violence and seeking first not the Kingdom of God but a United Ireland to the point of idolatry. Lord, before You and one another, we ask pardon for the pain caused to people in mixed marriages. Reveal to us, we pray you, practical ways of eliminating such pain. We ask forgiveness for contributing towards the rapid breakdown in values and break up of marriages, by our failure to recognise and expose unchristian values in our city.

'We confess these things and ask pardon from God and you, our Christian brothers and sisters, and resolve at any cost to contribute to Christian standards.'

The third prayer was entitled 'British Confession of Sin' and was read out by an Englishman, who stated: 'I repent of present and past sins of the British people against Irish people of both traditions, and especially the sins of pride leading to coercion; the sinfulness of laws which declared that an Irish-born person living among the Irish should be considered an evil person in the eyes of men and the law, and the whole attitude in mind exemplified by such laws, that has poisoned the centuries and that denigrates the Irish people; the action of armies and governments that killed and dispossessed Irish people, many of them living entirely peacefully in their land; the acts of Church and State in seeking to curtail the religious freedom of Irish people, Catholic and Protestant; the sins of neglect that ignored intolerance and discrimination in government and employment; the economic and social neglect of Northern Ireland, an avowedly integral part of the United Kingdom, leading to large scale unemployment and underprivileged and relying upon the solution of emigration.'

As we walked in silence with the cross through the city on that Good Friday, the sense was that God would honour this sincere decision, and would protect the city from violence, death and destruction for many months to come because of the repentance of the few. What followed was the longest period without violence on the streets of Derry for the seventeen years of the Troubles up to that point.

For me, this Word validated that this was the way; the two sides repenting publicly and praying for each other. Some people argued against it, asking how you can repent for others, for people who lived before you were born. Well, Moses repented on behalf of the people. I think you can repent for those who would have been willing to repent if they had been given good leadership.

On St Columba's Day, 9 June, that same year, some four hundred people stood in silent prayer outside the Guildhall, in Derry, many with a hand raised in prayer for non-violence in our city. The absence of any guns or tanks in the vicinity was a welcome response to our public appeal for no violence that day. Many churches rang their bells to remind the people of the city to join us in prayer of petition.

The prayer for me was also one of gratitude because since Good Friday, when we processed through the city carrying a cross and took part in a repentance service, there had been no violence in our city.

'Repent and believe the good news' is the original gospel. Repentance cleared the way so we could believe. When a person hurts you and you go to pray, all you see is their face sitting in front of you. Unless you forgive that person, you cannot pray. If you ask God's blessing on someone you are at odds with, you will get healing and reconciliation.

The Twelve Steps
We use the Twelve Steps model in the treatment programme at White Oaks Rehabilitation Centre, which I dedicate a chapter to

later in the book, as it has had a profound effect on my life and ministry in the area of true repentance and awareness of the power and grace of reconciliation.

I remember spending three hours at White Oaks one day with a woman who was doing her fifth step (finding another human being to whom we can confide the nature of our character defects and hurts). There were tears in her eyes when she came to me with what she had written and asked me if I would read it out. I told her to read it slowly herself and that she could take all day to do so, if need be.

The pain and the healing, and all that happens in the Fifth Step, convince me that this is one of the most Christian programmes I have ever come across. The power of God at work in these Twelve Steps is quite amazing.

There is reference to the person who has hit rock bottom in the Twelve Steps programme. You see life in the raw working in the rehabilitation centre. People may be abused at six or seven years of age, who cannot form a proper relationship for the rest of their lives. They are drinking and drugging to try and get rid of the pain. And yet, they can get better. That is the miracle. Once it is out, once it is talked and prayed about, and help is sought and counselling given, healing begins to happen.

The softness which repentance brings is not being experienced today. The Sacrament of Reconciliation is not being availed of. Perhaps, this is because it has become too much of a ritual. People focus on the sins they have to confess and not on the person towards whom they are repenting. Catholics were given a list of sins to confess as children and have not, for the most part, been able to find grown-up language to express the failings and wrongs committed in adult life. Believe me, Protestant guilt is just as real, especially in the area of drunkenness, as there is a great sense of shame and failure for people who have such problems.

The help that comes when addicts get a sponsor, or a confessor, to speak to is very much like the help a person gets after making a general confession. The added factor of sensing that we are forgiven by God's grace and our faith in God is a great bonus. Yet even for the person without faith, the fifth step of the Alcoholics Anonymous programme, The Twelve Steps, is surely a great help in recovering sobriety, and starting on the way towards contented sobriety and serenity.

We use a phrase in our constitution for the Columba Community, 'to joyfully repent', because repentance brings a joy. In other words, a child running back to his father does not go back with the sense of heavy obligation. He goes back with joy.

In the religious sense, 'Confession' placed the emphasis on confessing a list of sins, while 'the Sacrament of Reconciliation', understood properly, puts the emphasis on the one with whom you are being reconciled, that is, the Father.

It is a matter of turning away from sin to believe in the gospel. It seems to me that I will not turn towards that life unless I am aware of it, through praying before the living Word of God, before the light of Christ. We return towards a living God, a loving being. We give up something 'good', or what to our intellect appears 'good', in search of something better. Perhaps, the witness of another person well on the happy journey of recovery is the something better we will go for, when we meet that in another. As one man said 'whatever you have is what I want.'

I remember being on a directed retreat with the Jesuits in Manresa, Dublin, in 1986, and while I was sitting before the Blessed Sacrament I found myself weeping a lot. I told my spiritual director that it was as if my heart was being massaged. It was allowing the Lord to highlight for me His goodness and love, and that allows the dust to be seen, like when the sunlight shines through a window and allows the dust to be seen, the mistakes and faults to be admitted.

When I have stepped wrong, and come back and ask God's forgiveness, I feel His faithfulness in operation. Joyfully repenting somehow needs to be the experience if people are to be won back to the Peace of God.

These are some of the teachings of the community, as I attempt to outline what I mean when I refer to the central four characteristics of the normal Christian life, which are the pillars of the Columba Community's ethos and spiritually.

Listening prayer
The Columba Community, its employees, and beneficiaries, testify to one thing, which is the prayer of listening and waiting on God's Word before we move with any apostolate. For 'unless the Lord builds the house, they labour in vain who build it' (Psalm 127).

Listening prayer is central to a new, revived concept for the Church of the future. We cannot rely on man's good ideas for renewal of the Church. We must believe God wants to guide us with His ideas for rebuilding the Church and the Kingdom. We have had enough of a Church that has acted with heady pride and pomp, and I suspect many in church leadership today, in Ireland, are ready to listen humbly to the Lord's guidance. This will surely lead to a renewal of God's people on their pilgrim journey.

Over the past thirty-five years, if there is one thing that has been central it is our commitment to meet together for weekly prayer time and the business, or discussion times. We meet at Columba House twice monthly, and once monthly at St Anthony's and White Oaks. The meetings are led by a member of the community, who chooses the theme. Each year, we give teachings on the Baptism in the Holy Spirit programme.

At the times of silent listening, members and the public are encouraged to share any Bible text given to them in prayer. Sometimes we finish with small groups, where individuals may have private prayer ministry. Before the public prayer meeting, the community members meet to consider any business regarding one or other of our centres.

Christ's Peace Amid Conflict

I have been blessed in my wanderings and questioning over the years. I have seen the oppressed and materially poor man, through God's grace, become aware of the riches of the treasure within himself and of being loved by the Father, and become transformed as a result.

This is not in any way to excuse or justify the support of institutions that exploit the poor, but it is to offer a strategy for obtaining a just society. The strategy of the gospel of Christ is forgiveness. Genuine spiritual renewal is a prerequisite for the type of social reform and political change necessary, at home and abroad.

My eyes were opened to this truth during a stay in El Paso. While visiting in the dire poverty of Juarez, Mexico, just south of the Rio Grande, I learned a profound lesson on reconciliation. The exploited poor were the poorest I had ever seen. For days, I watched lorry loads of cardboard being driven south over the Rio Grande, from the United States, to be sold as housing material for the poor.

Amid such houses, we celebrated the Eucharist in the open air, with a ragged cloth serving as a canopy over the table. Firstly, the priest, Fr Rick, called his 'apostles' together. They were tough looking, poor men. These men were anointed with oil during the Eucharist. They took part with joy. There was a light in their eyes that betrayed their deep faith in the power of Jesus to reconcile, to heal.

I found myself weeping as I was being anointed by one of these men. I was privileged to be caught up in a mystery, the mystery of the very rich poor. Almost immediately after Holy Communion was distributed, these 'apostles' distributed food, bags of flour, only to the men who held shovels and appeared ready to begin work. The work, I later discovered, was building better housing on the edge of this 'Dump of Juarez', as it was called.

Fr Rick explained to me how, when these people had been 'baptised in the Spirit', the Lord's love and power of forgiveness in them became evident even to the rich merchants and shop-keepers. When the rich, materially speaking, experienced from the poor this new life of peace, joy and love, they also became influenced.

The poor no longer held the rich bound in their guilt, but freed them by their love and forgiveness. The rich, in turn, freed from their centuries old guilt complex, now began to share more of their wealth with the poor. It was when the poor became aware of their richness of spirit that things started to change for them materially.

It was then I realised the power of the oppressed, or those who think themselves oppressed, to free the apparent oppressor. This is profound. It is the power Jesus had on Calvary when He could influence the centurion who helped crucify Him, and say: 'Father, forgive them for they know not what they do.'

Over the years, especially after my own Baptism in the Spirit, I had a growing compassion for prisoners, and a desire to set captives free from all kinds of burdens and fetters. And so, in the seven years following the opening of Columba House, we visited prisoners and their families, and led a ministry of healing and peace building.

I felt more confirmed that I was on the right track when I heard Pope John Paul II speak about reconciliation in Phoenix Park, during his visit to Ireland in 1979. After this, I remember going up to visit the big cement cross at Fahan, in Co. Donegal, which had been erected by the men of that area in honour of the Eucharistic Congress in 1932. I climbed up Scalp Hill to it, with a young lad who was on his way home from school.

Come to think of it, those were carefree, innocent days when I did not have to hesitate before inviting this young lad along. Sadly, in today's world we are not free to even think about such an invite as a result of the abuse of children by adults, which has left us bound in our obsession with rules and regulations in the interest of health and safety. Necessary, when one considers some of the lives ruined by abuse, but also so curtailing of freedom and spontaneity.

Standing on top of the hill, looking out over the valley below we locally call 'the bosom of Fahan', where lies the ruins of the old St Mura's Monastery and the oldest cross slab in Ireland, I felt I was being asked by the Holy Spirit to erect a cross of reconciliation on the opposite Golan Hill, which overlooks my family home.

Incidentally, Fahan in Gaelic is *Fathain Mura*, which means 'The sheltered place of Mura', a Columba follower, some say a Patrician monk, who was the founder of the great monastery at Fahan, which shelters his inscribed ancient cross to this day.

This word I got was not as clear as the word that came to me 'to wait', which I mentioned earlier, but it kept me going when, for years later, I looked up at the mountain and saw the cross shining as I returned from journeys to Long Kesh prison in the evenings. For me, it was a symbol of Christ's victory. We call it the Cross of Reconciliation. It was the first step in building something new.

The Church of Ireland Minister in Buncrana, Canon Cecil Thornton and I blessed this cross on the first day of January in

1980, which I remember being a beautiful, mild, sunny day. I suppose we did it in honour of the Pope's visit and a call to reconciliation.

'Set the prisoners free'

In 1983 I wrote a small book called *Freedom to Captives,* which was an attempt to apply Christ's opening mission statement in Luke's Gospel to our own calling in Columba Community, to serve the marginalised or poor in our society. In those early days, some of us visited Long Kesh and Magilligan prisons twice weekly, celebrating Masses and leading prayer meetings. Every Thursday evening, on our return from the prison visits, we were greeted by a packed congregation for the nine o'clock Mass in Columba House for the prisoners' relatives.

At one stage during the hunger strike, which took ten lives in 1981, it became clear that men would continue to die in prison for what they believed in. I attended three of the hunger strikers, two died and one eventually came off the strike. I can only confirm how sincere these men were. Seeking guidance for me, and for our community, was essential if we were to be of any help to all the people involved in the hunger strike.

At that time, Fr Seamus Kelly asked me to offer Mass in St Mary's Church, Creggan, in Derry. Though the Mass was for the sick, and we prayed with and for the sick, I also asked for prayers for the prisoners and for the men considering hunger strike.

In the quiet time after Holy Communion, a strange mental image came to me. It was of a sheaf of harvested wheat. Behind this sheaf of wheat there was a very bright light coming from what I first observed as a cross. On second glance, I could clearly see that it was a two-edged sword, shining brightly on the golden wheat. Then it appeared that one particle of wheat was a serpent's head, and I could also see the clear shape of the serpent's body coiled around the wheat. It was only visible because of the strong light coming from the two-edged sword, which is the Word of God in Scripture; Christ, Himself, illustrating that what may appear as all pure is often infected by evil. This, certainly, was true of the stance and position of both the IRA and the British Government on the hunger strike issue.

Those who jumped on the popular bandwagon, via the media, to defend and support the idea of a hunger strike, in effect, helped to oil the conveyor belt that brought young men to their deaths. Other deaths also took place during the protests and counter violence that followed the death of the hunger strikers.

It became clear to all later that Maggie Thatcher, already bitter about the Brighton bomb and the death of her trusted friend, Airey Neave, was not going to give in to the demands of these prisoners to be treated as political prisoners. The fact that the British Government had, for years, already set and upheld a type of political status prisoner in the 'cages' since the beginning of the Troubles, surely was an encouragement to the men in the H-Blocks to seek the same status.

The point I wish to make, in telling the story of the vision of the word of God and the serpent of deception, is central in our community's position on the hunger strike. It is essential that, as believers in Christ, we seek together God's plan and work in our lives when we are faced with life and death situations. Too often we react in tribal ways, and without listening prayer.

The Spirit of Jesus wants to guide us in such grave matters, and in life's details also. As churches that have been slow to oppose wars, slavery and oppressions throughout history, we need at this time to learn that the Lord Jesus will speak, guide, if we are prepared to seek His face, and not just take up political positions that are driven by the ways of the world and knee-jerk reactions that result from our socialisation process and slant on history.

One Sunday afternoon, as I was leaving Long Kesh, a lady asked me to visit her relative, Mark, who was on hunger strike. She said that he wanted me to visit him, so I returned to the prison. It became the practice there to relocate the hunger strikers who were fasting for a long time. Mark was very weak and was due to die quite soon. When I entered the room where he lay I was shocked, not only by his state of starvation, but because I realised that I had met this man before.

Some two months earlier, I had been offering Mass as usual one Sunday with the H-Block prisoners. I had made it known since before Bobby Sands died that I was against the hunger strike. I was never in the habit of castigating when preaching in prison over the years, and had always tried to preach about Christ and His message of love and the Father's forgiveness. However, on this issue we had prayed a lot and, as stated earlier, felt the need to dissuade these young men from such self-harm, as it would lead to their deaths and to the deaths of others.

I usually got on well with the prisoners and had a laugh with them, but there was a sombre mood this particular Sunday, so after Mass I asked if anyone wanted to say something. I sensed that it was only fair to give them a say, although giving groups like this a platform for such a discussion was likely against the rules. It was an exceptional time, however, and tensions were running high, so most would accept that when it is a matter of saving life, rules take second place.

A young man from the group spoke up. He said: 'Father, I have always enjoyed your sermons. Today, however, you have made me very angry. As far as I am concerned, I do not want to see you again.'

And he got his wish, because as I entered his room some two months later, after he asked me to visit him on his deathbed, he was already blind. He reached out his hand in greeting and immediately thanked me for coming. Then he said: 'I'm sorry for offending you after Mass that Sunday. I have a bit of a temper.' I answered: 'That's alright. Join the club. I have that problem myself, so I understand it.'

He seemed content and smiled. I asked him if he would like Confession or prayer. He told me that he had already had a good Confession with the prison chaplain, but that he would be happy to have prayer. I recall asking what his expectations of the next life were and what he expected after death. I will never forget his answer: 'Heaven, for me, is to be up there watching the Brits withdraw from Ireland and know that I had a part in it.'

God alone knows how the agencies of our socialisation process form our conscience and mentality. God understands our conditioning and, while He wants Christ's peaceful, non-violent ways to prevail, He alone, with His great compassion, can be our ultimate judge, who will take in the total picture. He knows all the circumstances surrounding our formation and decision making.

So many countries in our world sadly put flag and fatherland before the ways of non-violent activism, as preached by Christ and practiced by his followers for over two hundred years after His Ascension. It is my firm belief that real strength and credibility can again be enjoyed by the people of God returning to those early days.

What a major shift that would be. It would certainly allow the Christian world to rotate on a new axis of liberation from the pseudo-political roles that we find ourselves operating presently, with the prevailing scandals that power-grabbing and materialism from a church involved with military has brought upon us.

Though I saw the hunger strike as morally wrong in itself, there is no way the word suicide could be used in relation to these deaths. Suicide involves two clear concepts. One is the bringing about of one's own death, and the other is culpability. The latter not only involves the intention of the person who dies, but also the circumstances surrounding his decision and how much of a choice, or how much real freedom, he had.

Those of us who attended the prisoners in their dirty cells, where they lived twenty-four hours a day for four years, know how demoralising these conditions were. It was at this stage that the strong Christian, in the negotiations for better conditions, would have succeeded in reaching a better solution. But who is strong or capable of bending when each side is harbouring guilt? Things could only get worse, and before condemning the decision of the hunger strikers one would need to have lived as they did for over four years.

The devil thrives in the deadlock that cries 'No surrender', and he wove his web of confusion over the land, at that time, in such a way as to have eminent men 'support the hunger strikers unto death'.

By our support, we can encourage all types of irrational behaviour. We do not even have to walk in marches or speak words of anger, as many did during the hunger strike. We only have to feel deep anger. We can generate life or death, energy or dissipation, hope or despair.

In a final effort to encourage a Christ-like solution, I wrote a letter to Margaret Thatcher, who had, after all, read St Francis' Prayer for Peace, 'where there is hatred, let me sow peace, where there is injury, pardon', the day she was elected Prime Minister of Britain.

Almost two months later, I received a short note in reply, from a junior official at the Northern Ireland Office, to state that my letter had been received, and that the 'Prime Minister had done everything possible to solve the problem regarding the hunger strike.'

I lived in Columba House at the time, and our small community of nine men included four ex-prisoners. We met daily for prayer and counsel, and, as members of the interdenominational Prison Christian Fellowship of Northern Ireland, we hoped to extend the prison apostolate to all Northern Ireland prisons.

We started two prayer and Bible study meetings in the H-Blocks in Long Kesh, involving thirty to forty men, and we witnessed many miracles of God's grace at work across the tribal or religious divide.

Fifty-Seven Days on hunger strike
One example of how the Lord brought these young men from death to life for His own purposes is the testimony of former Republican, Liam McCloskey, who had spent fifty-seven days on hunger strike. Sentenced to ten years in December 1977, for offences connected with arms, hi-jacking and armed robberies, Liam joined the blanket protest and then the hunger strike in Long Kesh in 1981.

During his time in prison, he started to read the Bible and religious magazines, which led to him wanting to find out what it was that made people love and serve God. He also began to pray, and first become aware of the fruits of prayer when forced washing began for all prisoners involved in the dirty protest.

Tension was high as the prisoners prepared to resist the washing, and, afraid of what lay ahead the next day, Liam knelt down in his cell and prayed, realising that the only one he could turn to for help was God.

It turned out that during the night the block OC had spent much time thinking over the situation, decided that it was in the best interests of the men not to resist, and so, first thing in the morning, he countermanded the order to resist.

With these events changing his whole outlook on prayer, helping him to realise that he was not strong enough to stand on his own, Liam found that at times when resentment and anger welled up inside him, reading the Bible always mellowed it.

He went on to learn to pray the Rosary, and began to say two a day on his own and another with the rest of the men on the wing who prayed, as well as saying other prayers in the morning and at night.

While Liam began to have many doubts about the use of violence, he felt unable to leave the protest as he felt close to those around him. So, when talks between the Northern Ireland Office and Cardinal O'Fiaich and Bishop Daly broke down, he added his name to the list of those prepared to go on hunger strike. Kevin, his cell mate, also volunteered and later died on the hunger strike.

When it came to his turn, Liam's conscience would not allow him to do anything else but to go on hunger strike, as to pull out would mean another man taking his place and, perhaps, dying. During his hunger strike, he continued to pray and reflect on his life. He came to believe that while he had hoped to do good for the Irish people through Republicanism, he had not succeeded in doing anything but wrong.

Having become increasingly weaker, Liam woke on the fifty-fifth morning of his hunger strike feeling so weak he thought he would soon be in a coma. His mother came to visit him that day, and told him that she could not have his death on her conscience and would take him off the hunger strike as soon as he went into a coma. His sight had already failed.

While his first thought was to keep going, he began to feel that it was unfair to leave these things in his mother's hands, so he decided to stop, and his recovery began. Liam was moved to the military wing at Musgrave Park Hospital and, after a powerful injection, his eye sight returned, but never like it had been.

As he tried to get his life into order, he realised that for too long he had been trying to serve the cause of Republicanism and serve God without succeeding in serving either. He tried to work out how to serve the Nationalist people without using violence, and eventually began to feel the pressure of what seemed like a raging battle going on in his mind. On one side was a strong urge to give himself totally to God, while on the other was a feeling of running away from the Nationalist people, from the men on protest, and from the men who had died.

In his mental anguish he called on Jesus and, from being drained in mind and body, he was revived. He read in the Book of Revelations: 'I know your deeds, that you are neither cold nor hot; I wish that you were cold or hot. So because you are lukewarm, and neither hot nor cold, I will spit you out of my mouth.'

He decided to end his links with Republicanism and try to follow the way of Jesus, and from that point he went on to experience more joy, beauty, depth and love than he ever knew existed.

On being moved to Magilligan Prison, in Co. Derry, at his own request so that it would be easier for his family to visit, Liam began a new way of life and took part in weekly Bible classes and fellowship meetings for all denominations, which helped them to understand and accept each other, while they all kept the beliefs in their respective denominations.

Members of the Columba Community and I helped to lead those meetings each week, and this was how we met Liam and others who joined us years later at St Anthony's Retreat Centre, when they were released from prison. Liam lived at St Anthony's with us for nearly five years and did great work for youth.

There was some concern among the Republican leadership when they learned that men were being converted to the Lord and turning away from militant Republicanism. Traditionally, prison has been a place where opposing forces grow harder in their convictions and ideologies, but the praying and Bible studies made a difference to some. I have letters from a lot of those men saying how much they felt blessed by the prayer meetings.

Prison fellowship

In the late eighties and early nineties, I used to travel twice weekly to Long Kesh. On Sundays, we offered at least two Masses in the separate H-Blocks, and on the Friday evenings I led two separate hour-long 'Bible classes', or prayer meetings there.

All of this got to the ears of some Protestant businessmen, who approached me about helping start a northern branch of Prison Christian Fellowship. Chuck Colson, the former Attorney General of Watergate fame, and an ex-prisoner, was the founder of the original Prison Christian Fellowship. After a trip to America and working for a month with this movement, I joined up as one of the founding directors of Prison Fellowship Northern Ireland. Sadly, it turned out to be a bridge too far.

When we attempted to start an interdenominational prayer meeting in Magilligan Prison, where many of the prisoners who were turning away from Republicanism had been transferred to, I was aware that some of the Catholic prisoners wanted to come to the prayer meeting, but were not yet at the point where they could cross the Catholic/Protestant divide or, more accurately, the Loyalist/Republican divide.

I suggested that maybe we could facilitate these people and help further the reconciliation process by having two united prayer meetings per month, and two meetings where Protestants and Catholics could meet separately.

This would have meant that those not ready to come together across the political divide would still get a place to pray. It was a question of applying the 'latitude of acceptance principle', well known to educationalists, that is, we do not teach multiplication before we teach addition. We must take one rung of the ladder at a time, and not push people beyond where they are ready to go.

The next day the Governor of the prison, a former Presbyterian minister, telephoned me and accused me of trying to undermine the integrationist policy of the prison. He told me that I would no longer be allowed into the prison and, when I tried to gain admittance, I discovered a red card in the pigeon hole allocated to me, barring me from all future admission. Of the hundreds of football games that I had taken part in, I assure you that this was my first and only red card. As noted elsewhere, the state authority can easily misuse its power when it realises one's vulnerability or lack of local church leadership support.

Pressure had also been building from a certain attitude at work in the prison, with some seeming to have difficulty respecting the fact that Catholics could be Christians. The situation was compounded by the fact that a Catholic, who took part in those prayer meetings, ended up being apparently proselytised by this more fundamentalist section. The Columba Community, and other well-meaning Catholic people, had no option but to withdraw our support and ministry from the Prison Fellowship in the mid-eighties.

Sadly, this young Catholic man, who became friendly with an evangelical medical doctor who visited the prison, was later killed. He was not opposed for his faith but for other alleged fraudulent activities. It should be said that the IRA were not too worried when anyone gave up being a member of their movement for religious reasons. They were more worried and fearful when other reasons were given for resigning from the movement, or if the faith reason was not genuine or was suspect. While IRA activists saw nothing wrong with bombing Protestant and Catholic businesses and putting people out of work, they knee-capped and killed people for what they referred to as anti-social and fraudulent behaviour.

So much for trying to serve the divided people, or divided church, in Northern Ireland. In a land where two people are poles apart, I suppose they view the one in the middle as being closer to the other side than to themselves. That imagery came to me while I was contemplating the entire work of mediation and the healing of divisions.

Looking back on that time of prison ministry, I can see how all the cracks in the 'body' were exposed and old fears, prejudices, hates and long-standing notions of each other emerged. I remember thinking that there had to be an immense shift in the psyche of Protestants in our country if they were going to love Catholics as Christians and, even more so, a Roman Catholic priest.

A young, ex-prisoner, who was a Loyalist, told me years later, when visiting the Columba Community at St Anthony's Retreat Centre, that he had hated me as a Catholic priest when he met me at the mixed prayer meetings in prison. He talked about a great weight being removed from his shoulders as he prayed for deliverance from the hate and anger towards me. We both then recalled that day in prison when we shook hands.

Strangely enough, I was aware of this young man avoiding me at the time, and we, in the Columba Community, had prayed for him just before we went to visit the prison on the very day that he experienced the change in his heart towards me.

I praised God at that time for those Protestant ministers who could openly embrace me as a brother. I recall especially Revd Cecil Kerr and Myrtle, his wife, who were friends I stayed with at the Christian Renewal Centre in Rostrevor, Co. Down. The charismatic style of the Christian Renewal Centre there allowed all shades of the Christian family space to pray, reflect, and discuss how much we all had in common. Indeed, the Charismatic movement, in the mid-seventies to mid-eighties, brought many of us together who would not normally have had a platform where we could unite and pray together.

I sensed the warmth of complete acceptance when it was there, and was pained by the coldness of its absence in other people. No amount of nice words or pleasantries can disguise the absence of brotherly recognition, and respectful acceptance of one's faith.

At one stage, I found myself questioning the source of my empathy with prisoners, particularly paramilitary prisoners. I wondered was it because the Spirit of Jesus was in me to preach the Good News to the poor and because He said: 'I was in prison and you visited me', or was it because I saw the prison population in my country grow by nearly three thousand in ten years, and felt deeply that the prisoners were a mere product of a violent society, a visible fester easily fingered on the body that contained the rottenness and poison within?

I came to see that God works through nature. He is not a sadist. He gave us knowledge and free will, and yet implants our deepest desires in our hearts. His hand is above all the circumstances that influence us when we seek Him.

When we say 'yes' to Him, He will build on what is good in us, and have our minds and hearts purified, and His deepest desire for us realised. He may do so in most unusual ways; through the hands of fearful or jealous men, or through the hands of good men.

The Columba Community came about as a response to a need in a city and country where more and more of our youth found themselves in trouble with the law. The effect of the Troubles on parents, wives and children had become obvious to the many dedicated, already overworked clergy and social workers in the troubled areas.

We need to be with the sufferers, even if he/she be an angry parent or prisoner who feels let down by the establishment. For this reason, our centre welcomed ex-prisoners and their relatives, and ran special prayer times for them.

The spiritual, or inner, awakening was often followed by the inner healing necessary before many of these young men could be free from the hurt, anger and fear that prevented them from being channels of Jesus' power, peace and love. Some had suffered severe torture at the hands of legal forces, while others had engaged in physical violence. Only in a loving Christian community, with prayer and counsel, could these memories be healed.

After thirty years of waiting, ex-UDA and ex-UVF members started coming to us with ex-IRA members, and wanted trans-generational healing through our 'healing of memories' programmes at our Sanctuary, in Muff, Co. Donegal. They wanted to work for the betterment of their families. For me, that was the ultimate fruit of the waiting and of God's work in that community.

While politicians have had more than their share of credit and praise for bringing about the Peace Process in Northern Ireland, in truth, the forgiving people, both Protestant and Catholic, who had lost loved ones during the Troubles, deserve thanks and due recognition for their major part in bringing about the Peace Process.

Often these are the forgotten heroes. These are the quiet soldiers of Christ, who worked daily and prayed for the forgiveness and change of heart needed for any genuine power sharing and healthy society to operate.

We meet them all over Ireland, north and south, in small gatherings of Catholics and Protestants, who humbly have admitted their side's contribution to the problem and are more than willing to contribute towards the solution.

I could tell many stories of individuals from both sides of the divide who took heroic stances, after being graced with a special spiritual or religious experience which allowed them to have much more compassion for the other side.

The prison work was one of the very few apostolates that I was welcome to be involved in. Apart from the Carnhill parish, where Fr Seamus O'Connell was the parish priest, and when Fr Michael Collins would invite me to the Long Tower parish, I was seldom asked to say a public Mass locally.

So, offering Mass practically every week in Long Kesh was always an option to praying with my own small community. The other option, which I often responded to, was giving retreats and days of renewal around the country.

The festering sore in Ireland

For some thirty-five years now we, in the Columba Community, have worked and prayed for reconciliation. In particular, our small community has promoted healing of wounds and reconciliation for people in Ireland. Some, especially in the south of the country, have given the impression that the problem of strife and division, or the conflict known as the Troubles, is solely the fault of the people in the Northern Province, who live 'over the border'.

With this in mind, I recall being asked to speak at a conference for peace in Co. Wexford when the violence and killing by both sides was rife. I stayed with a priest friend of mine, Fr Aidan Jones, for a few days while preparing for the talk. I had plenty of material to speak about, but felt the need for a fresh view, or new insight, on solutions to the Troubles.

After a time of prayer, I went for a jog on the beautiful beach at Courtown Harbour. It was then that I received a vision, or mental image, that has stayed with me, and has allowed me and others deeper insight into how violence and, indeed, political or institutional violence, is supported. Often the supporters of violence are not really conscious of what they are doing.

The image that came to me was of a man's torso. The left shoulder of this body was badly wounded, bloody and festering, while the rest of the body seemed clear of such ugliness or festering wound. The image spoke loud and clear. While the visible festering, bloody wound is located in a particular part of Ireland, the North East in particular, clearly the entire body is affected and sick. The entire body, therefore, must take the medicine for healing – the antibiotic. The medicine, if we are to have a holistic view of the entire body, must travel through every vein in the body.

The medicine is repentance and prayer for forgiveness, as well as work for justice and peace. This is the antibiotic that will cleanse the entire body. Only when we stop blaming the other side, and begin listening to their fears and the cause of their anger, will they in turn begin to respect us and, indeed, examine their own reactions. Pointing the finger, or adding to the pain in the festering part, is not going to help.

This Christian teaching is confirmed by St Paul's inspired teaching on the unity that exists in the mystical body of Christ. It also makes good psychology, as the blame game only serves to scapegoat, vilify, or demonise the other. This is especially true when we begin to blame the prison population from the Loyalist and Republican working, or workless, class in the North, as if they were the sole cause of the Troubles.

Often these ghetto areas are, indeed, problematic, but are also the results of a policy of former greed, exploitation and dominance. We empower the negative and the evil by projecting the entire blame for the Troubles on to one part of the country, or to one section or social class, instead of looking for ways we can contribute towards a solution.

South African visit

Writing just days after Nelson Mandela's funeral, I am conscious of how his philosophy or spirituality of life influenced South Africa and, indeed, peace-loving people all over the world.

He was in some ways the Ghandi and Martin Luther King of South Africa, who influenced his people to include 'the other side' in negotiations for a better future. He did so mostly from a prison cell. One wonders would he have survived or, indeed, have had such a positive influence had he not been imprisoned for all of twenty-seven years. God's ways are strange and have ways of purifying such men.

I visited Johannesburg and Soweto just before apartheid ended. As part of a Masters in Peace Studies, at the University of Ulster, I did my thesis on Northern Ireland. I was interested not only in the comparison between Northern Ireland and South Africa in general, but in the use of bad religion, in particular, to help foster differences and division. From those studies in the early eighties I recorded some strange contributions from clergy, which undoubtedly fostered bigotry.

A Jacobite minister, writing home to England from The Cape, wrote about the local native black Hottentots, and said: 'These people do not communicate like human beings. They communicate the way chickens make noises. If they have a Heaven it will be the Heaven that animals go to.' This particular tribe has a click sound in their vocabulary and language which certainly sounds unique.

Talk about setting the stage for exploitation and apartheid. The colonists needed to first paint a picture of a decadent and ignorant people who had no culture, before they could, with any conscience, impose their brand of oppression and slavery under the guise of civilisation, or education. One has only to look back at the London-based newspapers to illustrate how the Irish people were portrayed in a similar way. Thank God we have moved on from those days.

One memorable visit to an area in Johannesburg was quite eerie. Had I not been through the barricades in Derry, and prayed in homes during the wakes of IRA members, when the masked comrades of the deceased stood looking on, I would likely have been scared.

I had been invited by some Dominicans to dinner, with relatives of mine, to meet a famous priest called Fr Albert Nolan. I had read his book, *God and South Africa*, and was fascinated by his work in engaging such a large cross-section of Christian religious preachers and leaders. He was on the run for a while from the authorities because of his views, but gradually was listened to.

When we met, he was staying in a Dominican house which was more like a fort. The Dominican brothers, black and white, lived in an area where the entrance was via a manned iron gate. Inside, the atmosphere was one of generosity, joy and hospitality. I recall Fr Nolan saying that he had more hope for peace and harmony in South Africa than he had for peace and goodwill existing in Northern Ireland. Given the current continuous wrangle and lack of agreement on issues like flags, drums and marches, I think I know what he meant.

I was also invited by a friend, a Dr Newman, to attend a Peace Corps meeting where the Mandela party, the African National Congress (ANC), was in negotiations with the local members of the Inkatha Freedom Party (IFP). They were surrounded by the all-white police, who were the tallest group of men I ever saw. They all looked to be at least six-foot-five.

During the intervals, it was interesting to have the freedom to speak with activists from different sides. Many of them told me that they had been trained in Russia in the ways of guerrilla warfare. I met one white army officer who trained with the British army in Northern Ireland and knew well the area on the border where I came from. It certainly is a small world.

On the lighter side

When I left the Cathedral parish in Derry back in late autumn 1978, I stayed for a week or so in Our Lady of Bethlehem Cistercian Abbey, Portglenone, Co. Antrim. I knew Fr Martin, the guest master there, from his visits to charismatic prayer conferences, and, since spending that time in the abbey, he and his fellow monks have always made me welcome.

Some years later, in the early eighties, Fr Martin wanted me to take him to Long Kesh to help hear confessions. On the way, he asked me to stop at a shop and buy him about twenty packets of cigarettes, and as many bars of chocolate. Though it was a very hot summer's day, and I was dressed in a short-sleeved clerical shirt, Fr Martin wore a large gabardine overcoat and proceeded to load all the cigarettes and sweets into its large pockets.

Just before we entered the prison, I reminded him of the top security that existed in this notorious institution. He smiled and told me not to worry. I felt sure that he would be refused entry and told him that I would leave the car door open so that we could meet up there afterwards. However, something amazing happened after that.

When I was searched thoroughly and had handed in my car keys, I moved on along the corridor trying to look back as casually as possible at Fr Martin. We were asked to stretch out our arms, so that the prison officer could search our bodies and clothing from elbow to ankle. There was six-foot-three Fr Martin, with his hands stuck into the pockets of his open overcoat and stretched out like a batman figure. He was felt and searched from elbow to ankle alright, but walked into the most securely guarded prison in these Isles with two pockets loaded to breaking point.

I went into one H-Block wing, and he went up the diagonally opposite wing. I had not reached the second cell before I was asked for a cigarette and then chocolate. When I answered that such items were not allowed, the prisoner told me that the other priest had been distributing them. Later, when we met up at the centre of the H-Block, the smell of cigarette smoke was in the air, but no comment was made.

On another occasion, Fr Martin thought that he would give some prisoners a treat for Christmas, but that did not work out so well. I have met some cool people over the years, but none as calm and cool as Fr Martin. When I spoke to him about including this story in my book, he was as gracious and light-hearted as ever. Few priests have done more for young men and their families caught up in the Troubles than he has.

Days of reflection for the RUC

During the years of doing retreats on the theme of forgiveness and healing, as well as leading prayer meetings in prison, our community was always supported by the monks of Portglenone. Indeed, in the early days, when I was without finance, Fr Martin collected from some of his better-off friends to help us rebuild Columba House and other places.

We held retreats for Catholic members of the RUC during those troubled days. With the support of Fr Celsius, his Abbot, Fr Martin hosted a few retreat days during the mid-eighties with the help of a retired police inspector from the Waterside, in Derry, which proved very beneficial to all concerned.

This was a new experience for me. It was one thing to preach the gospel to prisoners, as I understood for the most part where they were coming from. It was quite another thing to address the RUC, even if they were Catholics, as I had to deal with the stories told by my parents, as well as the evidence caught on camera of the behaviour of this force, now called service, during the early part of the Troubles in Derry.

However, as these men came to Confession, and we had open discussions after the talks on healing, forgiveness and ways of possible reconciliation, I began to understand them, and found them to be men and women of sincerity. Only when we can listen with respect to both sides in a conflict can new ways forward be developed.

Fr Martin and his friend, Danny McDaid, a retired policeman, like many unsung heroes, did their bit towards the peace we now enjoy in our land. It occurs to me that while some politicians got the credit publicly for bringing about the peace process, I know of many who worked and prayed a lot to allow this climate to prevail. Somehow we, the people, have not been allowed, or have not taken the opportunity, to celebrate that. Part of the reason for this, is that we sense the present peace is an uneasy one based on political expediency.

When we continue to wrangle, and spend precious time and money on the flag and marching issues, it is proof that we have not come near the peace Christ speaks of, where our security and primary identity is based on love and not fear of each other.

It occurs to me that we could do with an Albert Nolan, who exposed bias and error in the so-called Christian teachers of South Africa. We need a well-researched book of a similar kind, entitled *God in Northern Ireland*, if we are ever to expunge the error and hate that underlie the attitudes of many of our northern people.

Efforts are being made to develop a more accurate and

respectful understanding of each other's real beliefs and values, but much more is needed. Perhaps the Irish School of Ecumenics could produce a simple catechism outlining our position as Christians, and illustrate how much we have in common. It would be a start in addressing the misinformation and vilification of the other that has been the legacy of many past generations.

There is a lot of talk nowadays about addressing the legacy of the past, which refers to the thirty years of physical violence and terror. I would suggest that the term should at least include the story from the time of partition. It should include how people's minds have been poisoned when the Catholic religion in particular has been demonised.

I worked in parishes in Scotland for eleven years and was once spat at by a complete stranger. On another occasion, I was deliberately and heavily shouldered just because I was wearing a Roman collar and dressed as a priest. I would be surprised if any Catholic, church going or not, would ever treat a pedestrian Protestant clergyman in that manner. Surely, leading clergy in the north need to admit that this level of hate and bigotry exists and do more to deliver their people from this, if we are to have respect and true peace in this place.

A trip around Ireland

Reconciliation has always been to the fore in the prayer and work of the Columba Community. This does not exclude the mentioning of situations that have brought about division and misunderstanding. Yet, it is essential that we recognise both God's blessing and power to bring us beyond our conflicts.

Around 1989, I was part of a group of four – two Catholic priests and two Protestant ministers – who went on a trip of reconciliation around Ireland. Along with me were Joe Petrie, a Methodist from North Carolina, Norman Ruddock, a Church of

Ireland minister from Wexford, and Frank McCloskey, another Catholic priest from America, and we travelled around fourteen prayer meeting centres in as many days.

Before we left to go anywhere, we met for tea and a short period of prayer in Columba House. After that, a discussion started as to whether we should bring one car or two. I sensed that this question might come up as one of the ministers did not get along with one of the priests. It was simply a personality thing. Anyway, I excused myself in the middle of this conversation and asked the Lord to direct this important decision.

In the few minutes' silence that followed, I distinctly heard the word 'opulence'. Having returned from the kitchen, Joe said to me: 'Neal, you are our appointed leader for this mission. What do you think about us using two vehicles for the trip?' I said: 'Opulence', to which Joe immediately replied: 'That is a word from the Lord.' It certainly was from the Holy Spirit and a word not used much in my vocabulary. So, off we went in one vehicle.

We started in Letterkenny, and then went on to Magilligan Prison, Belfast and Armagh, where we met with Cardinal O'Fiaich. It was an eventful trip, with many laughs and some tears. By the time we reached Courtown Harbour, in Gorey, Co. Wexford, we were aware that we were talking for too long during the prayer meetings we attended. Everyone wanted to share a little, so it was decided that ten minutes each was enough, except when we all discerned that the Holy Spirit was anointing someone in a special way at a particular time. It was then agreed that if one of us spoke over the ten minutes, the rest would either not speak or be very brief. To ensure this brevity, we agreed to let the speaker know when to stop by one of us lightly tapping his foot on the floor.

Revd Norman, God rest his soul, was the first to speak, while the rest of us sat in the front row of a crowded church. No sooner did Norman finish quoting a Scripture to start his sharing than I tapped my foot on the floor. He started laughing, and when he explained what had happened the entire congregation laughed heartily with him. That was a great night of joy, which we were all refreshed by. Our good friend, Fr Jim Gogley, the parish priest of Courtown, enjoyed the fun also, even if, like the parishioners, he did not know the reason for the origin of the laughter.

When we got to Cobh, on our way to Cork, quite a bit of tension had developed due to a clash of personalities, especially between the American priest and Revd Norman. I was hit with a twenty-four hour bug and could not attend the prayer meeting that night. Instead, I went to bed early at Oliver Broderick's House. Oliver was a leader of the prayer meeting.

Praying for the others and the group that night in bed, I received a strange vision. I could see Norman and Joe arriving through swinging doors into a big hall, where the group of about thirty people were praying. The group was situated in an adjacent corner of the hall. Fr Frank was standing up talking and Norman called out 'Halleluiah', as he was wont to do when in good spirits. This upset Frank and the unity of the group.

The next day, as we packed to move on, there was tension in the air, to say the least. Standing at the car, I suggested that we pray for forgiveness and healing for what had happened the night before. I described what I saw in my mind while at prayer the night before. At first, one of them asked if I was told all of this from our host, Oliver. When Oliver confirmed that we had not shared any of this and that I had not seen the hall, the mood changed, and we all realised that the Lord was asking us to be as one if we were to continue to preach a retreat around Ireland, about the need for reconciliation with God and with one another.

Reconciliation and working together as denominations has always been important to the Columba Community. Presently, I work on a daily basis with Revd Joe McCormack, who does great spiritual work with the clients of White Oaks. We need each other more than ever in Ireland these days.

During that trip around Ireland, Fr Frank told me a story. A man was learning to play golf and was swinging, but missing the ball for a while. Each miss resulted in his taking large divots of earth from around the area of the ball. He did not realise that he was wiping out hundreds of small ants from an anthill beside where the ball lay each time he swung at it. Eventually, there were only two ants left. One turned to the other and said: 'Mate, if we are going to survive this, we better get on the ball!'

Sounds like a good motto for the divided church.

Footsteps:

Our Pope Has Died

Footsteps, once again, are heard
at early dawn
on cobble stone streets and pavements.
Like steady drums they beat their way to do him homage
as he leaves for home.
It does not seem like quarter of a century ago
since that sound awoke me.
It was towards Phoenix Park that we converged that day.
He came among us. He kissed our ground.
He spoke God's word. He sowed the seed that would bear fruit.
And even if an enemy came
and sowed cockle that would also grow.
We will always remember His word,
his plea on bended knee for justice, yes,
but for non-violence and for freedom from hate.

Now his voice is heard again.
It sounds more loudly now in its silence from his window.
In our weakness is God's strength made manifest.
In man's brokenness the Light of God shines forth.
We all witness this paradox,
If we have faith to see the power of the cross.
This symbol of defeat and death
is also the symbol of hope and victory for the true Christian.
God give us the grace to surrender to its meaning,
for when the Son of man comes will He find faith on earth?

Golan Hill Cross

*25th anniversary of erection of Golan Hill Cross
of Peace and Reconciliation*

Death, as we look on this dark, but shining cross,
we ask you,
where is your sting?
For us who believe,
fear hangs on the cross
defeated by love.
It is finished.
Increase our faith in You,
Risen Lord Jesus.

Healing the Sick

Looking back on over thirty years of ministry in the Columba Community, and previously in parish ministry at St Eugene's Cathedral, praying with the sick has been a major work. The faith to experience the Lord healing as we pray over people by the laying on of hands is a gift, yet, it is a gift to develop.

We, in the Columba Community, pray always with faith. Jesus could not help many people in Nazareth because they did not have the faith in Him. When we pray for healing, we pray for spiritual, emotional and physical healing.

Often, the Spirit will give mental images as we pray to encourage and strengthen faith and trust, both in the minister and the patient. I remember one time praying with a lady who was worn out with morning sickness during pregnancy. She had already had a couple of miscarriages, including twins dying in her womb. She had the remains removed, but only after a couple of weeks did she realise that the surgeon had left one dead child inside her, not realising that she had been pregnant with twins!

The understandable anger with the hospital because of this serious blunder only served to add to the weakness and pain that severe morning sickness was causing again during this new pregnancy. She was desperate to retain her pregnancy this time as she had no children, and had constant morning sickness which left her sick.

We listened to her and then prayed. I found myself praying firstly for some understanding and forgiveness for the medical people. Then, in praying over her in tongues, the mental image of a brewing teapot became clear, which I found strange. I told her then that we were going to have a strong cup of tea and that I sensed she was healed of her severe problem. At first, she protested but ended up drinking the tea and eating a sweet biscuit. She still speaks about that day of blessing. That was nearly thirty years ago and I have met her once since, about five years ago. I remember shortly after she was prayed with, a man stopped me in the street. He introduced himself as the husband of this lady and thanked me for whatever I did for her, saying that she had not been sick since. He also told me that he was not a practicing Catholic, but was very grateful to God.

Mrs Donna Laird, from Derry, has told the wonderful story of her healing from breast cancer at some of the talks the Columba Community is invited to give from time to time. She had found a lump on her breast but was afraid to go to the doctors, as her mother had died with breast cancer two years previously. She was hoping that the lump would go away, but when it did not, she plucked up the courage to make an appointment with her doctor.

Confirming that there was a lump there, the doctor told her that with her family history she would be fast-tracked for an appointment in the hospital. She got an appointment for the following Wednesday in Altnagelvin Hospital, in Derry, and on the Monday night before it she came along to the healing Mass in St Anthony's with her sister, who had telephoned me to say that they were coming.

Donna remembers me praying for the fire of the Holy Spirit to come down on the congregation, and when I finished praying she felt a severe burning pain where the lump was, which took her breath away. When Donna's sister asked her what was wrong, she told her that she felt she had been healed.

After Mass, I indicated to Donna that I would pray with her, and she told me that I did not need to pray over her because she had been healed. She then told me what had happened during Mass, and as I prayed over her I could feel the energy coming from the healing she had received.

When Donna went for her appointment at the hospital, the doctor examined her and, finding a lump, sent her for a mammogram. However, when she went back to get the results of the mammogram, the doctor told her that he could not understand it, but nothing had shown up. She has gone on to lead a healthy life and is the mother of two children.

On another occasion, in a remand home for young women in the Newcastle Diocese, in England, I had a crowd of young people to pray with, but we were short on time. I suggested that they come in and pray and listen. One of the first to come in was a fifteen-year-old girl. I put my hand on her shoulder and I got this mental image of a bathroom, the door of which was locked. I asked the girl if she had ever locked herself in a bathroom and she started crying. Then she showed me her wrists, and told me that six weeks previous she had locked herself in the bathroom and slashed her wrists. The Holy Spirit was telling me what the problem was. The Spirit often allows the person's pain or problem to present, or surface, much faster than the normal counselling process would do.

During the writing of this book, Columba Community member, Ann McCay reminded me of a healing she had received in the mid-seventies. She had been attending the charismatic prayer group which met in St Joseph's Boys School, in Creggan, and had developed a very large sore on her skin in the centre of her neck, at the front. It was red, raw and ugly. Periodically, a crust would form over it, fall off and then reform again. This went on for quite some time and she became increasingly worried and self-conscious, and as a result she began to wear a light scarf, loosely tied around her neck, to hide the sore from view.

She was attending the doctor regularly to try and find a remedy, but nothing she was prescribed worked. One night, at the prayer meeting, she spoke to me about it, and I told her that I was going to Knock and would pray that it would heal over and dry up, and that the crust would shrivel up and fall off.

When I returned from Knock, Ann told me that the sore had done just that, dried up and healed over, and that the crust had shrivelled up and fallen off. It never returned. Praise God.

A good friend of the Columba Community, Ted Armstrong also recalled a healing he received in the late seventies. He had been suffering from a slipped disc and, from time to time, was enduring very severe pain.

From being a placid and confident person, he had become nervous and vulnerable, being terrified of being jostled while walking, clinging to his seat in buses and at times experiencing blinding pain while driving.

I had been aware of Ted's condition and, at a parish Blessing of the Sick, I prayed over him. A few days later, at a day of renewal in Thornhill College I prayed over him again.

Ted began to feel more confident and slowly became aware that he no longer felt vulnerable. Within a week he felt much better and, in the following weeks, he became more and more certain that he had experienced a healing, and gave thanks to God.

Praying for healing by proxy
During an all-night vigil at Columba House a lady and her husband arrived to ask me to pray for their son. He'd had a serious accident and, some time previously, had an operation to stop bleeding around his brain. Apparently, the internal bleeding in his skull had started again. This time the doctors were considering operating through the upper part of the patient's mouth in the hope of stemming the blood leak. The operation was scheduled to take place the morning after the couple visited me.

When I prayed over the mother for the young man, then already in the hospital, I received a strange, but clear image. I could see children playing out in a snow-covered lawn, and the date, 25 December, was also very clearly seen. I recall telling the parents that I thought their son would be home and well for Christmas.

I realised that this was a strange thing to say, given that Christmas was a short time away. However, the image during the prayer was so clear and I felt very positive about the outcome.

The next day, when the couple went to the hospital they were met by the sister overseeing the proposed operation, who told them of her surprise a short time earlier when the surgeon decided to postpone the operation. That morning the blood leak in their son's head had stopped. I later enjoyed a visit to this family's home and, indeed, witnessed the heavy fall of snow on Christmas day.

Healing and the Holy Eucharist

We, as a community, always tie in healing with the Eucharist, and we pray with people for healing after Mass every Monday and Thursday night. When someone asks for healing, we need to remember through whom healing comes. 'By His wounds we are healed' was Isaiah's prophecy about the Risen Christ. It is Jesus who heals, not us, and this is something that we need to get into our heads. There is always the danger that we misplace the glory.

The Eucharist is the source and apex of all spiritual activity. Jesus is present in the Eucharist, and the faith to believe in that is everything. 'Go forth, your faith has made you whole', said Jesus. I have had the experience of people coming for healing and I know they are examples of living faith.

The last passage in Mark, 16:15–20, sums up what Jesus wants to leave with us: '… and the sick upon whom they lay hands will recover'. The whole purpose of Christ coming, dying and rising, is that He wants to live in an incarnate way in us. If we believe that the Lord is within us and we lay hands on people, we do so in His name and with His blessing.

I attended a man in Altnagelvin Hospital who had drunk enough weed killer to kill a man twice over. Interiorly, I heard someone say to me that that was not going to happen. I went up to the man and put it to him what he had done. I told him that the doctors did not hold out much hope for his recovery. Then I said to him: 'Medically speaking you would die with the amount of weed killer you have taken. However, I am sure the Lord is going to heal you', and when he was tested again there was no trace of the poison in his blood or urine.

What happens if you pray and nothing happens? I think that is why a lot of priests do not pray for the sick. Every prayer is heard if we are men and women of faith. It may not be answered in the way, with our limited vision, that we ask for. If we are asking for something that is God's will, then it will be done.

There are a number of reasons why I got into praying with the sick. I recall being chaplain to a group that had travelled to Lourdes, and I remember looking at a gathering of people in wheelchairs and wondering how they could be happy. I was good at athletics, and loved running and being physically fit, but I could see the joy and serenity in the faces of these people and their sense of purpose. The blessing was that the Lord was present with them in their suffering.

As I stood at a vantage point during the procession for the sick that day in Lourdes, the people that I saw in wheelchairs were so serene and at peace that I just could not stop weeping. I was wearing a grey, clerical shirt and I slipped my clerical collar into my pocket, hoping that nobody would realise that I was a priest. I would not care today, but then it was bad enough to be a man weeping, let alone a priest.

I often wondered why those gentle, vulnerable people in wheelchairs at Lourdes had such an emotional affect on me. Looking back, I think that I paid a great deal of attention to being very physically fit as a young priest. So much so, that I could not understand how anyone handicapped could possibly be happy, or content. The Lourdes experience, together with caring for and praying with the sick and handicapped people that I have been blessed in meeting ever since, have taught me different. Age has also helped me to have a more mature and Christian view on sickness and weakness, generally.

For those who are in wheelchairs, when the Lord touches them it is a spiritual healing; they get to accept their cross. That is a great gift. Lourdes helped to give me a new appreciation of the dignity of weak human beings, and how important faith in Christ crucified is, if we are to remain loving and at peace in times of trial and illness.

Just recently, the Columba Community engaged a local professional film-making team to produce a documentary of the history of our existence over the past thirty-five years. One of the interesting areas of our work which attracts people is our prayer for healing, which takes place at St Anthony's and at Columba House, at the weekly healing Masses.

We prayed that people who were healed would come forward for this part of the documentary and several did. Among them was a lady called Denise, who reminded us that she had been off work as a waiter at her uncle's busy restaurant because of back injury. At one point, the back pain was so severe that she was on morphine.

She recalled how Marie McCormack and I had both prayed for her in the upper room after Mass one Monday night, at St Anthony's. As we prayed, she 'went away', to use her own words, and later recovered consciousness while lying flat on the floor. This posture, apparently, would have been out of the question for her for two years beforehand. She got up from the floor and never felt pain or ache in her back ever since.

Denise was, in fact, 'resting in the Spirit', which is a state some people go into during prayer for healing. I have had this happen when praying for the sick. Frankly, we do not encourage this for a number of reasons, principally because there are people who seek this experience for its own sake and for sensationalism.

However, in cases like that of Denise, it was the way the Lord chose to bring her to have healing in her back.

Thinking about that particular healing, it occurs to me how important it is to have two people pray, rather than one, for a variety of reasons, health and safety being one of them. Again, Jesus was the man of wisdom in all of this, as he appointed them to go out two by two to preach the good news and to heal the sick.

Among the many stories relayed to members of the Columba Community over the years is the following one of a young boy who attended the healing Mass in St Anthony's when this book was about to go to print. I thought I would use it to conclude this chapter on healing. It affirms my belief, borne out by experience, that the Lord honours the faith of little children. They are so open and trusting.

My name is Gareth McLaughlin, aged nine years, from Carrontlieve, Fahan, in Co. Donegal. I have had breathing problems all my life. When I was eight, I got very sick and could not breathe without coughing. Every two or three breaths, I would start coughing and coughing. This went on from early morning to late at night for four weeks.

My parents took me to the doctor and, over the following weeks, I saw four doctors, had many medications and visits to the hospital, but I did not get any better and missed a full month at school.

I remember one cold, wet Monday night, my grandad and mammy took me to a Mass, and a priest took me close to the altar and prayed over me. When I awoke the following day, my coughing had stopped. I went back to school the next day.

My family and I believe that it was the healing Mass that stopped my coughing and cured me, and I would like to thank Fr Carlin and God.

I often recommend to parents that they pray with their children for healing, even when the child is asleep.

Feast of the Holy Family

The Holy Family are refugees hounded by Herod. They are the first basic Christian Community. They do 'what they think God would have them do and humbly rely on God to match calamity with serenity' (*Big Book of AA*).

In White Oaks, our rehabilitation centre for the treatment of alcoholics and drug addicts, we see the pain of broken family relationships.

John was quite a typical alcoholic. He presented for residential treatment in his mid-forties, estranged from his wife and children, angry and embittered. 'This Higher Power, God thing' eluded him.

He was a thinker whose feelings were messed up, so love relationships with God and others were impaired. Prayer, the language of love in the heart, was impossible. Impossible, that is, until he spoke of his estranged father, who was also an alcoholic and living in a mental home, and whom he 'hated' and had not visited in seven years.

We got to pray to Jesus to heal the memory of that key time when John was eleven years old and the drunken father embarrassed and hurt him deeply; then the floodgates opened.

Tears poured down the cheeks of the wounded child. He was crying from the heart for love and to express love. Life was restored for John, his family was restored, and father and son were reunited.

John could dream again like Joseph. John could love again and could pray again. Jesus' needs reintroduced to the pained families in our land.

St Anthony's Retreat Centre

A humble 'Bethlehem' place

When our prison ministry eased up, the Community focused on the development of St Anthony's Retreat Centre, which opened in 1985, and this is where I have lived ever since. Some members of the Columba Community also spent years living there, as did some ex-prisoners.

St Anthony's, like Columba House, was strongly influenced by our Community's interest in our Celtic Church roots. We believe that modern society can learn a lot by looking at the lives of some of our local saints, such as Columba, Mura and Egney, who had a rich tradition of monastic life combined with hospitality and evangelisation.

I would like to pay tribute to Columba Community member, Marie McCormack and her pivotal role in developing St Anthony's as a retreat centre. Before she retired from teaching, Marie trained with the Jesuits in Dublin and at Portadown, over a few years, and became a qualified spiritual director. She turned out to be a gifted director and, before having to retire due to illness, gave guided retreats to clergy, religious, and lay people alike, using Ignatian spirituality. This allows the retreatant to move at their own pace by use of scripture, prayer and reflection.

I celebrate a healing Mass in the oratory at St Anthony's every Monday night and, over the years, many people have come along and experienced spiritual and physical healing. Marie joined me in praying for many sick people, and great results followed. She taught us how to use the spiritual exercises in our own journeys, and how best to assist others who would come for a few days' retreat.

As a very central, and founding, member of the Columba Community, Marie has been a great positive inspiration in my life. She lived at St Anthony's during the early years, when a few of us roughed it without much comfort. We prayed under poor light as we had our power from a windmill at first, then progressed to a generator and, finally, after nearly two years, we were able to afford to get electricity conveyed to the hill top, where it had never been before.

Marie developed Parkinson's disease in the late nineties. However, as that progressed she also had to have a heart by-pass, which added to her trials and frustration due to memory loss. She bore all this with courage and with amazing acceptance. Some years later, she had a brain bleed and would have died only for two of our community members and friends, Tommy and Ann McCay, who called to her door to take her to the community meeting.

Marie was unconscious for some five hours and, after brain surgery for a burst aneurism, has been in a nursing home ever since. We visit her at least weekly and are amazed at her quiet, humble spirit being still very much intact. When she prays in the spirit, she continues to thank God for all kinds of blessings. I often think that if there was ever an argument for learning to pray and for contemplation, Marie is it.

It is sad to see someone once so central to the school where she taught, and to our community, now incapacitated. It has been for me, and others, a lesson in letting go of someone so dearly loved. I needed to accept that she now has a need of full-time care, albeit among strangers, who do their best but do not know the person I have known and loved over many years.

The climb of Golan Hill on 1 January 1980 to erect a Cross of Reconciliation. Pilgrims included, on my right, Cecil Mitchell, a shopkeeper from Fahan, Co. Donegal, on my left, Revd Cecil Thornton, Church of Ireland, Buncrana, and Ted Armstrong, principal of St Joseph's Secondary School in the Creggan, Derry, where I had been chaplain.

A ceremony in the Guildhall, Derry in 1988 to dedicate the three Christians Together Repentance Crosses that were to be used in the repentance services in London, Dublin and Belfast. Standing with me at the front is Sr Aloysius, Catherine Montgomery, Revd John Lappin and Joan Tapsfield. Back row, Ron Desmond, Liam Lynch and Diane Lampen.

The Christians Together walk on Good Friday 1985, when the cross was carried from Columba House, through the streets of Derry for a repentance and confessions service in the Guildhall. Representing the four main churches locally, from left, Revd David Gray, Revd Alan Harper, Revd Neal Carlin and Revd Liz Hewitt.

Talking at a Prison Fellowship Conference in Belfast in 1983.

Gathering wood for the fire during the early days at St Anthony's.

Members of the local community of Drumhaggart who came along to help out with the renovation work at St Anthony's in 1989.

No way through! The back road to the border between the North and the South was closed off during the Troubles, blocking access to St Anthony's Retreat Centre.

Chatting with Revd Norman Ruddock, Church of Ireland, at the opening of St Anthony's Retreat Centre.

Brian Stewart (left) , Tommy McCay (right) and I examining what we called 'The Dragon's Teeth', at the blocked road leading to St Anthony's Retreat Centre, during the Troubles.

Bringing home the turf. Patsy Barron, with members of his family and friends, delivering turf to St Anthony's Retreat Centre.

Bishop Seamus Hegarty with Columba Community members at the opening of the Celtic Prayer Garden in September 2006. Seated, from left, Helen McLaughlin, Mary T. McDonald, Isobel Harley, Ann McCay, Marguerite Hamilton, Kathleen Devlin. Standing, from left, Mary McCauley, Christine Doherty, Marie McCormack, Brendan Carlin, Fr Neal Carlin, Bishop Hegarty, Maurice Harron, Tommy McCay, Ann Cavanagh, Irene Cosgrove.

Cistercian monk, Fr Martin, Portglenone, and Bridie Quinn, of the Portglenone Prayer Group, with Columba Community members, Marie McCormack and Kathleen Devlin, at the Celtic Peace Garden in 2006. From the early days Fr Martin was a great supporter of me and the Columba Community and he still keeps in contact.

Columba House staff and volunteers at the launch of the YARD project and the refurbished Columba House in 2011.

White Oaks Rehabilitation Centre staff and board members with the award received in 2012 from CHKS, which is the equivalent of the Health Information and Quality Authority (HIQA).

The official opening of
the Sanctuary.

My mother, May, sister, Angela, and brothers, Dessie, Aidan, Dermot and
James, joined me at St Columba's Church, Long Tower, for the twenty-
fifth anniversary of my ordination to the priesthood in May 1989.

Enjoying a chat with Monsignor
Joey Donnelly and Liam
McCloskey during the celebration
of the Columba Community
receiving Canonical Acceptance
into the Derry Diocese in 1995.

Marie is much loved by the entire staff of nurses and helpers. She always has a kind word for each member and they tell us gems of conversation that still shine through, amid her wanderings. Her Christian spirit continues to be very much in evidence and she thanks each of us for every visit. Her awareness of being a teacher of confirmation classes, and a teacher of spiritual truths, emerges now and again, as if from a hidden treasure.

In some very mystical way, we sense Marie, like many good people who are now ill or old, teaching the rest of us how to accept what cannot be changed. As the poet, Milton wrote about his impending blindness: 'They who best bear his mild yoke, they serve him best. They also serve, who only stand and wait.'

When Marie joined us in the early eighties, she spoke a lot about St Anthony of the Desert and about a possible hermitage for some members of the community. It is not surprising that she and community member Kathleen Devlin were instrumental in bringing us the Good News, in words they received during our usual all-night New Year's Eve vigil, as we prepared to welcome in 1984 and prayed about finding the right place for a retreat centre. The Scriptures were about prayer and a lonely place, the tilling of the land and the need for personal renewal. We felt that the retreat centre should be in a quiet place in the countryside.

Then, a few days after the prayer vigil, I went to Dundrean, near Burnfoot, on the Derry–Donegal border, to thank a man who had made a donation to Columba House before Christmas. When I arrived, the man's wife told me that he was working at land he had bought, as it was advertised for letting out. When I asked if it was near the border, she told me that it was right on the border between Derry and Donegal. She directed me to it and, there and then, the man offered me the old farmhouse and extensive garden for the retreat centre. It was a blessing.

When we came to see it, hanging on the gate was an old, tattered, plastic-covered calendar with a picture of St Anthony of Padua holding the Child Jesus, and so we named the centre after him, and also after St Anthony of the Desert, to whom we have great devotion.

He was one of the first great hermits who lived for years in the desert in Egypt. He lived an austere life, praying and doing penance, and many people came to him to get God's Wisdom. The eastern desert tradition he epitomised greatly influenced early monasticism. He inspired Celtic spirituality, and his image appears on some of the old High Crosses of Moone and Clonmacnoise.

The farmhouse was dilapidated. It had a tin roof and old Stanley cooker. For a few hundred pounds, we bought a windmill and generated our own power, but a storm later blew it to pieces. With the help of local people, the farmhouse was restored and four hermitages were built to provide accommodation for retreatants. One of the first people to help form a community there was Liam McCloskey, who had been on hunger strike in Long Kesh in 1981.

I remember some time later we had a machine digging up the yard outside the retreat centre and, one day, it unearthed an old crockery bottle, which had been buried about three feet down. The bottle was embossed with the words, 'Neal Carlin & Company 1840', which had been the wholesale Wine and Spirit Merchant business owned by my great-grandfather in the Waterside, Derry, and I took it as a sign that I was meant to be there. I still have the old bottle as a relic of those days.

St Anthony's, along with Columba House, became the cornerstone of our ministry. It is a God-send to all of us who enjoy tranquility, space, privacy, time and a place to pray and listen, and go for long walks in some beautiful countryside.

Every Christian who seeks God through prayer is confirming a tradition that began with the Desert Fathers and Mothers of the fourth and fifth centuries. Simple peasants, who contemplated spiritual progress, inner peace and self control, wealth and poverty, patience, humility, hospitality and obedience, would receive direction from learned monks and learn Christ's ways.

A philosopher once asked St Anthony of the Desert how he could be enthusiastic when the comfort of books had been taken away from him. He replied: 'My book, oh Philosopher, is the nature of created things, and whenever I want to read the Word of God, it is usually right in front of me.'

Cross border talks

There are many happy and eventful memories as well as difficult and sad ones that I could recall from those early days at St Anthony's.

By the late eighties, border security was intensifying. The British Army had already constructed large concrete blocks on the border side roads to stop all vehicles using them. One day the army completely blocked the road leading to St Anthony's. It was impossible to even walk over the border at this point, unless one was athletic enough to climb the nearby ditch at the side of the road.

When some of the soldiers laughed at a few women who were struggling to get passed the blockade to get to St Anthony's for the celebration of Mass, I decided it was time to do something about it. I telephoned the Brigadier of the army who was in charge of the troops in Derry, and read out to him the statement I had prepared to appear in *The Derry Journal*, a local newspaper, a few days later. It was entitled, 'Penal Laws back in Ireland – British Army blocks pathway to Mass at St Anthony's.'

That was a Friday, and the next morning an urgent meeting took place between us at the crossing in question. It was a strange scene. There, on a very wet Saturday morning, was Tommy

McCay, a leading member of Columba Community, and myself on one side of the border fence, and the army leader, with a member of the Northern Ireland office, on the other side.

The brigadier was in agreement with us that the blocked crossing was out of order and, the next day, had his men erect a bridge over the blockade so that people could at least walk over the monstrosity of a barricade. This was still a very inconvenient construction as it prevented, for example, cycling to and from Derry. Sr Sheila, who lived here at the time, often cycled to Mass at nearby Ballymagroarty, in Derry.

I recall the army representative telling us that he was a Catholic, and that his father had been given some honour by the Pope for his work in India. Tommy asked him what his father did. Apparently, he was an engineer and had built some important bridge. This left an opening for Tommy to ask: 'Would your father be proud of this construction?' as he pointed to the steel barrier.

This episode resulted in my being invited to have dinner at the Ebrington Barracks, in Derry, where the army was stationed in those days. There the brigadier seemed proud to introduce me to some young Catholic army officers educated by the Benedictines, as he was himself. I sensed that, like many in the army, this officer was given the impression that the trouble was between Catholics and Protestants, and did not seem focused on the real cause of the Troubles, which was, and is, political. Admittedly, when we listen to someone with the rhetoric of Ian Paisley, it must be said that this has promoted anti-Catholicism, and has contributed to the violence and hatred of the Troubles.

Breaking down wall of division
The other memory that springs to mind is the day these blockades finally came down, and the border roads were re-opened. John Major was the Prime Minister at the time. He took a brave and

courageous step in removing the blocks. I will never forget that day, as it was as if we had planned the readings and liturgy at Mass for that afternoon.

We were hosting a retreat at St Anthony's. The readings were the regular ones for that Sunday. One was from Isaiah about 'the rough ways being made smooth'. The New Testament reading that day was about the unity in Christ. It was from Ephesians chapter two, and read: 'It is he who is our peace, and who made the two of us one by breaking down the barrier of hostility that kept us apart.'

To hear these readings, while listening simultaneously to the steel pounding on and breaking down the barricades, just a few yards away on the border road, was an experience I will never forget. It was one of those days when belief in providence, or the hand of God in our lives, was easy to accept.

St Anthony's has always been for me a place where possibilities and dreams can begin to be realised. This quiet place has provided for many retreatants over the years, and has become an oasis for Columba Community members, our auxiliaries, and members of the public.

Indeed, White Oaks Rehabilitation Centre, which has existed since 2001, had its origins at St Anthony's.

The retreat centre became a refuge for some who had been ejected from the cities of Derry and Belfast. In the words of one Derry priest, 'Neal Carlin and St Anthony's Retreat Centre have become travel agents for the Provisional IRA.' This organisation literally gave the address of St Anthony's to 'hoods' and so-called petty criminals. The choice was either to be put out of the North or to be knee-capped.

We had people come here with addiction problems, and we quickly found out that we were not qualified to deal with them. Given the callers we had at Columba House, and our own experience of similar people at St Anthony's, we began to reflect seriously on the need for a rehabilitation centre. We asked ourselves if we, the community, were to help answer this need.

One of the more light-hearted stories about God's guidance, as we discerned it, is this. We were fasting and praying regarding a possible outreach to alcoholics when I received a telephone call. The caller was reporting what he regarded as a great mishap. He told how the lady receptionist in Columba House, who was a volunteer, had become frightened when answering the door to a woman who was very drunk.

When the volunteer closed the door, which contained a large, stained glass image of Columba, the drunken woman proceeded to put her large boot through the stained glass window whilst shouting: 'Nobody ever listens to me!' As I listened to this story and reflected on it, I wondered if God was saying something to us. The hand of God may well have been in this, whatever about His boot.

This story, together with other promptings we were getting, eventually led us to seriously seek a place to minister to addicts and their families, and, in 2001, we opened White Oaks Rehabilitation Centre, which, twelve years later at this point, has treated one thousand, four hundred and thirty-seven residents and their families. As we will see, the Christian ethos, with which we minister professionally at White Oaks, has rendered very good results.

The primary reason for St Anthony's was to give people an experience of a retreat. There are now five purpose-built, en suite hermitages named after the four Gospel writers, Matthew, Mark, Luke and John, and Colmcille, where retreatants can stay and get in touch with their inner quest, the experience of the Spirit of God within and the Spirit of God in nature. It is also an opportunity to get guidance for a more fulfilled and generous life.

Personally, after sitting quietly and getting replenished, I feel I have more to give and, in return, I feel happier. People who have fallen out with the Church need to fall in with God. They need to go to the well of the living water to get replenished. Unless we get in touch with the fountain of living water, the source of our joy and inner peace, we will not live fulfilled lives.

Many years ago, I heard an engineer talk about how he had lost faith in the church for a time. He later spoke about a friend of his who asked the question: 'Imagine you were dying of thirst in the desert and the only clean, cool water you could get came to you through an ugly, twisted and rusted pipe. Would you take that water?' Of course he would. As Peter said to Jesus, when asked would he also go away like some of the previous followers did: 'Where can we go? For you have the words of eternal life.'

The Church is filled with frail, fault-filled sinners, yet God seems to choose to work through frail humanity. Accepting help, grace, and blessing, wherever you get it, seems to me to be the answer.

What we offer at St Anthony's is mostly taken from Ignatian spirituality, which is essentially applying short Scripture texts to wherever you are on your own walk. Inspired by Scripture and our Celtic Christian tradition, we created a pilgrim garden there with secluded areas for quiet prayer and reflection, and there is a little stream of spring water flowing through a Celtic Cross, which lies flat on the ground.

The spring, or well, gives us pure, clear water. It comes from a spring which rises on a plateau between two valleys; hence it is uncontaminated from anything overlooking it. The field next to it has never been ploughed or used for crops for many years. I see this fresh spring as symbolic of a fresh start for all of us who are seeking a church full of life. In fact, this stream rising in our garden is five metres from the border ditch and it becomes the borderline between the Republic and, politically speaking, the north of Ireland, all the way to Bridgend.

For me, the renewal of the Church could well be served in us returning to models as laid out in our Celtic heritage; a semi-monastic model. I think the Irish Church is called to finish the unfinished Cross of Kells, to build on the faith of the men and women of the Golden Age and their lifestyle.

Scripture tells us: 'Return to the rock from which you were hewn', 'Return to the quarry from which you were dug'. That is what the Celtic Cross lying across the stream of spring water in the garden at St Anthony's is saying to me; go back and look at the simple life of your ancestors. Many of these saints gave up positions of honour and riches to joyfully spread the Good News of salvation announced by Jesus Christ. Places like St Anthony's and its garden can help us divest ourselves of a clericalism that the future Irish church does not need.

It was from this quiet place of reflection that the idea of the Celtic Prayer Garden and the White Oaks Rehabilitation Centre had their origin, and were developed. We all need quiet places where our souls can dream dreams and get the courage to make them happen.

In the light of the above, I recall some years ago, before we were canonically recognised by the Derry Diocese, two Australian priests arrived for a week's retreat. One was the vicar general of a diocese and the other was a parish priest in a large city. When I asked why they had chosen to come here, I was encouraged by the answer: 'Well, we wanted to see what the Lord was doing in the Church in Ireland, so we are visiting the margins, as we think we will learn there what the Spirit of God is up to.'

When Bishop Seamus Hegarty came to the Derry Diocese, he arrived one day on the street at St Anthony's. As he emerged from his car, he said: 'You certainly live on the margins!' It was a loaded phrase, and we both knew he was not just referring to the quiet, country location, just a few yards from the state border that separates the Republic from the North of Ireland.

We had lunch that day and we talked. He asked me if I would come back into the diocese and I asked him if he could tell me why that never happened seventeen years earlier. He returned a few weeks later and, as we walked the country road along the border, he told me that he had made enquiries from a good section of the priests and also the former bishop. He said: 'Nobody has anything against you.' As we stopped on the road, I recall saying: 'Seamus, isn't it a strange church we belong to? I've worked out here for the past seventeen years as a priest, with the help of my local community and independently of the Diocese of Derry. It is now, with gratitude, that I and the Columba Community accept your invitation to be officially part of the diocese.'

I recall agreeing to trust Bishop Seamus as a person. With hindsight, I have learned so much about my own personal call to serve, and how to work best with the system, which at times can be intransigent.

Speaking about the church and its faulty human side reminds me of a story. Fr Bob Faricy, SJ, had just spoken at a charismatic conference in Belfast. As he and I walked together on the road outside the conference hall, we were approached by a man who was quite angry. I suspect in Northern Irish terms he would have regarded himself as a Christian. He shouted: 'Sir, your Church is the whore of Babylon.' Bob quickly retorted: 'That may or may not be true, but she is still my mother!' The case rests.

In summary, I have come to believe, on this journey of discovery, that, no matter how imperfect, or sometimes good, the system is, God rules. The sincere seeker is ultimately led on a path of inner peace and holiness, even when the cards seem stacked against him or her. In our community, we have developed a saying, 'God's hand is above all the hands that attempt to control our lives.'

He has His way when we learn to trust Him in those delicate areas of conscience, where laws and unbending systems have outlived their usefulness. Each soul, however, while free to soar on high, needs also to have healthy respect for the laws and regulations on the way up.

The Shepherds See the Light

Christmas Day Reflection

The powerless, as Jesus later pointed out, are they 'on whom God's favour rests'. The shepherds, like the sheep, lived rough. In their uncleanliness, they were looked down on by the Pharisees, yet God chose them to be the first to hear the glad tidings of great joy (Luke 2:10).

The weak, the despised, the poor, the sick, the dying and, indeed, the sinner who knows he or she is a sinner, seemed to be favoured by God incarnate. Is it simply because they are open and humble and powerless?

The Lord seeks to be born in the manger, in the outhouses of our lives. He cannot enter the overcrowded hearts and overactive minds. These do not reflect on what this time is all about. Where we are empty, open, vulnerable and in need, that is where Jesus chooses to be born anew in us. Later, He will mix with sinners and publicans. They will be called a Holy People, the Redeemed.

They say Christmas is for children. In truth, it is for the childlike; for the soul who gazes at the crib with awe, wonder and joy, with childlike faith in the miracle that God is with us.

The crib becomes a palace, the shepherd becomes an evangelist, and the earth becomes sanctified and purified, the stars, reflectors of the Light of God shining on earth.

The hymn, 'O Holy Night', says it all and all we can do is fall on our knees and all we can say is *cead mile failte romhat a Iosa*.

The Word made flesh lives among us. May His peace and ways be with you.

Outreach Centres

White Oaks Rehabilitation Centre

It had always been one of our main ambitions to develop a full scale, Celtic Prayer Garden, based on the tenets of the Golden Age of Ireland from the fifth to the twelfth centuries, when saints set up centres of prayer and reflection in remote areas and found God in nature around them.

However, this plan seemed to get waylaid when we realised that we should first focus on establishing a Rehabilitation Centre for those suffering from alcohol and drug abuse. The original call was always to be with those in the margins, so when the prison population decreased we started to discern a new ministry in the nineties.

In the course of our work with those both at the margins and the core of society, the community had become increasingly aware of the acute, and often hidden, problems caused by addictions, mainly alcohol. We often had men stay at St Anthony's who needed treatment for addiction, though they would present as seeking peace or spiritual direction.

In time, we concluded that the greater north west of Ireland needed a centre which would look at addiction, its causes and its consequences, and offer help in holistic and effective ways. I saw the centre very much as being for spiritual renewal, with an integrated programme of prayer, counselling and physical work forming part of the healing process.

With the support of ministers from other denominations, we explored the possibility of establishing such a centre and bought thirty-five acres of land at Derryvane, in Muff, Co. Donegal, in 1999.

Just like with Columba House, the land was purchased with money from a friend of mine who trusted that it would be paid back, and it was. There were a lot of challenges but we kept praying and White Oaks Rehabilitation Centre opened on the border, between the North and South of Ireland, in 2001.

The aim of the interdenominational centre was to draw Christians together, from different cultural and denominational backgrounds, to join forces in caring for those suffering from addiction to alcohol, drugs and gambling.

The centre was opened by Bishop Seamus Hegarty on the Feast of Michael the Archangel, 23 September, and is proving to be one of the largest outreaches the community has ever undertaken.

Over a decade on, it has built up a very good record in long-term sobriety and has been commended by British-based accreditation body CASPE Healthcare Knowledge Systems (CHKS) for its achievements.

We were delighted and encouraged at the eight commendations made by CHKS, which is the equivalent of the Health Information and Quality Authority (HIQA), in comparing White Oaks against their internationally recognised framework of organisational standards.

This led to us being invited to an awards ceremony in London, where we received recognition for two of the commendations, which were the centre's clear commitment to holistic, patient-centred care, and achievements in ensuring that a spiritual service is provided that encompasses all faiths and cultures.

The purpose of the centre is to aid the recovery of people suffering from addictions, and it does that for clients by improving their well-being and independence, and by addressing the core nature of their addiction problem.

It has been such a joy to see people and their families helped. One comment that has stayed with me is that of a young man who said that he had not been conscious of a life of happiness without alcohol and drugs prior to coming to White Oaks, but that after a year of sobriety, he could not possibly think of a life of happiness except without drink and drugs.

Many people think that the work of treatment centres is getting people off alcohol, drugs, or whatever their addiction is. However, the real way of succeeding in this is to get the person to think in a new and positive way, through becoming aware of their blessings, their real dignity and the potential for a happy life.

We tap into their willingness to achieve that. Many people are willing to make the sincere and genuine effort to get that new life, and if they are not, they certainly will not get it.

I believe the spiritual support offered to residents is one of the major contributory factors to the success of White Oaks, and is essentially what has been practised for years by members of the Columba Community, some of whom lead meditation at the centre a couple of days a week.

Here, I would like to express our appreciation for the contribution of Revd Joe McCormick, Kathleen Devlin and Marguerite Hamilton in particular. Over the years, on a weekly basis, these good people have contributed greatly to the success of the outcomes of the White Oaks Centre. Revd Joe, formerly Presbyterian minister in Burt, Co. Donegal, has now retired to Kilrea. Joe and I have developed a deep friendship over the years and have been together in this work since we opened the centre. Kathleen and Marguerite, who is now the principal of Thornhill College, at Culmore, continue to give inspirational meditations at the centre.

When we opened White Oaks in 2001, Marguerite took a career

break from teaching and managed the centre for two initially difficult years. I, personally, have had exceptional support from Marguerite's wisdom and spirituality. The Columba Community is also ever indebted to Marguerite for her generosity in using her administrative and spiritual gifts to build up the Kingdom of God in this area.

At White Oaks, we strive to provide a homely, stress-free environment, that is conducive to recovery, and we have delivered our thirty-day residential treatment programmes to one hundred and forty-four clients annually since opening.

Based on the Minnesota 'Twelve Step' Model, the programme incorporates intensive group and individual therapy, as well as family involvement twice a week, which is an essential part of the ministry at the centre. Focused therapeutic work involves activities such as sewing, art, yoga, gardening and music therapy.

After completing residential treatment, clients then attend two years of continuing care meetings weekly, which are facilitated by a voluntary service which is invaluable to the success of the programme. Indeed, the whole service offered by White Oaks depends critically on voluntary service, and we empower those in recovery to form part of the rehabilitation team.

The treatment programme at White Oaks is also linked with the Acorn Project, which we launched in 2001 providing employment through the promotion of organic produce, fruit, flowers and vegetables

The organic produce is sold at the neighbouring Visitors' Centre, which was built to serve the Celtic Prayer Garden that we went on to develop.

Medallion day
Perhaps the greatest day at White Oaks each year is what we call 'Medallion Day'. On that day, our ex-residents and their

supportive families come together for an afternoon of celebrating sobriety, and all that this new life brings.

Each ex-resident, sober for one or more years, receives a medallion imprinted with the three words from the Serenity Prayer – courage, patience and wisdom.

A priest who had spent all his working life in England as a hard-working pastor came to one of our Medallion Days, and I could not but notice his tears of gratitude, as person after person, on receiving their medallion, spoke of getting their lives back at White Oaks.

The 2012 Olympics had just taken place in London. While holding up his medal, one man stated: 'I sincerely mean it when I say that this means more to me than an Olympic Gold.'

Hundreds of men and women who were powerless over the addictions of alcohol, drugs and gambling, and whose lives and relationships had fallen apart, now had begun to live a happy life.

Thinking back on the challenging idea of building this two million euro centre some fourteen years ago, I must say that, at times, I thought it would take my life. Now I can say, with all the members of my community, that this work has given me new life.

It is important that we never allow fear of death itself to prevent us from giving new life. Certainly, it is in giving that we receive.

IOSAS Centre and Celtic Garden

Almost as a reward for giving up the dream of building a Celtic Prayer Garden and concentrating, instead, on helping people in a very practical way, it turned out that the land White Oaks was built on had an ideal space for just such a garden. The God of surprises who has a holistic plan for all of us will never be outdone in generosity.

As we walked around the six acres of natural heather and admired the mix of trees and wild bushes, we realised that we had stumbled upon an oasis of peace and tranquility, in what used to be a no-go area, not because it is located right on the border, but because much of it contained concealed water holes and bogland.

This provision both amazed and delighted me. Some fifteen years prior to this, I was inspired to contemplate the possibility of creating a map of Ireland on land near the border. The idea of representing the charisms of the Celtic Saints of Ireland in a pictorial way haunted me. I saw in this not only a revival of a memory of the Golden Age, but a way of enabling our youth to experience their rich heritage and faith as Irish people.

Some of us, back then, formed a committee and even went so far as to seek funding from Interreg. A number of obstacles presented themselves to frustrate that attempt and, on reflection, this was a good thing. More importantly, a good, praying friend of mine, Eugene Boyle, who helped me in the initial plans for this book, gave me a powerful and relevant Scripture reading at that time. The reading was from Habakkuk 2:3, and states: 'For the vision still has its time, presses on to fulfilment, and will not disappoint; if it delays, wait for it, it will surely come, it will not be late.'

As I took a look at this bog area at Derryvane, my neighbours said: 'This old swamp will be no good to you.' However, at that moment I recalled Eugene's prophetic words, and saw the possibilities and God's Plan for that garden.

Inspired by the Celtic spiritual renaissance in Europe from the fifth to the twelfth centuries, we wanted to develop a space that would offer therapy, serenity and healing, while preserving the garden in its natural state as far as possible.

The focus at the centre of the garden is the Trinity Circle, with different areas around the perimeter based on Croagh Patrick,

Brendan's voyages, the Island of Columba, St Brigid's Hermitage and Cross, and the Oratory of St Canice. We also wanted a few small lakes, the cave of Columbanus, and a shrine to honour Dympna in the European site.

Laid out in the shape of the island of Ireland, we envisaged the Celtic Prayer Garden evolving as the IOSAS (Island of Saints and Scholars) Centre.

Two pieces of Church history have always inspired me. One is the Acts of the Apostles, in which is detailed the faith, courage and community lifestyle that existed among the early Christians.

Acts 2:46–47 tells us: 'Every day they continued to meet together in the temple courts. They broke bread in their homes and ate together with glad and sincere hearts, praising God and enjoying the favour of all the people. And the Lord added to their number daily those who were being saved.' What an image of shared new life in Christ our Saviour.

The other piece of Church history that inspires me is the Golden Age of Ireland, from the fifth to the twelfth century, when hundreds of saints, such as Columba, Brigid, Enda, Kevin and Kieran of Clonmacnoise, built small church communities, giving place names to Ireland's townlands and villages.

They also evangelised and revitalised Britain and the rest of Europe. They brought the light of the living Lord and dispelled the Dark Ages that followed the collapse of the Roman Empire.

For many years, I had dreamed of a prayer garden to honour the men and women of Ireland's Golden Age and thus glorify God, and to renew interest in the characteristics of Celtic Spirituality, so that we, using them as our model, will be renewed.

Today, the church in Ireland needs to present the treasures of the faith in Christ Jesus in a way that will give life to our people, young and old. We need new wine skins to present the new wine of the Spirit of Love, Truth and Joy. We need renewed structures to simply present the fullness of Christ and His message. We need an Iosa-centred Church – a Jesus-centred community. I feel that the Lord is building new, authentic Christian communities.

Through the beauty of nature and reflection on our saints' gifts, the IOSAS Centre garden offers the opportunity for new life, especially for our hungry youth.

The Columba Community, built on the charisms of Columba (Colmcille), is an example of a modern Christian community of prayer and reconciliation. In such communities, the spirit and teachings of Vatican II documents are being implemented in a very real way. This model of Church, which requires by its very structure lay participation and is open to respond to the needs of our age in apostolic ways, certainly requires the attention of anyone seeking to live a full Christian life.

If we are to have the credibility, accountability and confidence of searching people, it would seem that alternative systems of governance, like the ones that Columba and his contemporaries had, are required.

Through the lives and ideals promoted by our predecessors, I pray that the Lord will inspire our people again, especially our searching youth, so that they experience the light of Christ and become light-bearers in renewed Christian communities throughout this land.

Still serving the local community in prayer, reconciliation, healing and building community, the Columba Community continues to address the legacy of the Troubles by encouraging people, from both sides of the divide, to take part in dialogue and programmes which will empower them to move on in their lives.

In progressing with our outreach to individuals and groups in our society who seek peace and serenity, we developed The Sanctuary Project at the White Oaks complex. Through this, we have provided residential facilities and a conference-cum-community hall to allow groups to come together in a private, confidential space, in order to tell their stories and help find healing and reconciliation.

As well as accommodating aftercare services for former residents and their families of the White Oaks Rehabilitation Centre, the Sanctuary is used for community relations projects, 'Healing of Memories' programmes, retreats, youth activities, male spirituality, community and creative arts, and events that promote peace and reconciliation.

Located in the Donegal countryside a few miles from Derry City, this border sanctuary is an ideal location for people from all over Ireland, and beyond, who like to get away for a few days' quiet reflection.

The Sanctuary is the perfect follow-up to the prison work of our Columba Community of Reconciliation. It complements all of our services for recovering people, and our work of healing for groups and individuals.

The more recent and exciting work with young people at Columba House has involved Derry youth also using the Celtic Prayer Garden and the Sanctuary facilities at the White Oaks complex.

The YARD project

The Columba Community felt a need to reach out to youth and their families, so this was something we prayed about. One morning I woke up with the word 'YARD' in my mind and we went on to develop the Young Adults Reality Dream project, with funding from the International Fund for Ireland.

Based at the newly-renovated Columba House, the project started in January 2010 with the aim of supporting young people and their families with the difficult issues facing them in today's society.

As well as offering support in the areas of addiction to alcohol, drugs and other addictive behaviours, the project addresses literacy and unemployment problems, through providing essential skills and links to other courses and employers. It also provides spiritual guidance and self-worth programmes, and support for parents and families of young people at risk.

Within the first two years of being set up, over one hundred and sixty people attended the YARD programme, 'Back 2 Ur Roots'. This involves sessions on drug and alcohol awareness, betterment of health, coping with addiction, spirituality and meditation.

Many are benefitting from the great work that goes on in the YARD project, and there have been a growing number of referrals from local general practitioners. As well as trying to help young people at risk, we have a family support day for families of anyone who is living with an addiction.

From an educational viewpoint, two hundred and sixty qualifications were attained by people involved in the first two-and-a-half years of the project. These qualifications were in youth work, information technology, peer ministry, film and video production, and conflict transformation.

While people get involved in the project to get a qualification, we find that by the time they are finished they want to develop their spirituality.

There is a Friday Night Club for young people that has a spiritual theme, and, with the Search Youth Group, we ran faith-based summer schemes called *Mol an Oige*, meaning 'Praise the Youth'.

In keeping with our call to reconciliation, we have a project called 'Challenging the Conflict', and through this we have built up good relations with young people at Clooney, across the river in the Waterside.

In its first two years, the YARD project touched the lives of over one-and-a-half thousand young people and their families in some way. Dreams are being realised. People are getting qualifications, with young people returning to full-time education having dropped out prior to being involved with YARD.

Presently, we are building on this by facilitating an early evening Tuesday youth project. While the spiritual awakening of the individual is a priority in this initiative, we would see new members of the Columba Community coming from this group. Young people who have been given the spiritual tools that helped form our community.

Just recently, we have joined forces with Youth Initiative (Y.I.) to promote Christian renewal for young people all across the city of Derry. As I watch this take root, I cannot but recall how fifty years ago I was involved with setting up youth clubs and athletic clubs, as well as teaching Religious Education in secondary schools.

Strange that the Lord had me travel the full circle, as we are again involved with youth, albeit much has changed in society. Needless to say, I and the older members of Columba Community are not as involved personally in the youth work, except to give it all the moral, prayer and financial support we can.

At the core of our being
each one of us is a saint
and that's what God sees.

Come Lord Jesus

The theme of this reflection is an invite to the Lord Jesus to come into our lives, to be born again in each one of us who says this prayer – 'Come Lord Jesus' – and means it.

Certain conditions are needed for this prayer to be answered, one of which is that we are serious about it and that our minds are not cluttered up with cares and worries, for we worry and fret about so many things.

Another condition is that our hearts are free and not full of inordinate attachments, such as addictions or behaviour patterns that we refuse to give up. We need to be free of resentments if there is to be room for Jesus in the inn of our heart, or we will be like the innkeeper saying: 'There is no room for you here. Try somewhere else. This is not a good time for you calling here.'

If we are serious about the invitation, 'Come Lord Jesus', we need to *repensare*; to think again, confess and be prayed with for forgiveness, and enjoy new life.

The Prodigal Son

It is only now, having squandered my gifts of body,
mind and spirit,
that I admit my wrongs.
I am sick of being sick
and following my own selfish ways.
These ways of wine, women and quest for happiness
have yielded misery, poverty, debt and ill health,
as well as a litany of offences and hurts to others,
especially those people whom I was supposed to care for.
Truly, I have sinned before Heaven and before you,
my Father and my God.
I have sinned against my brothers and sisters.
In the past, I excused my behaviour.
I was young. I was spoiled. I may have blamed my upbringing.
I may have blamed my environment and said:
'Everyone drinks too much in our society.'
I was, perhaps, not as good in school as my talented elder brother.
I had many excuses, but the fact is that caring for others
was a low priority.
Now Father, I want to leave this mire
and return to my own home.
Even now, I can recall memories of your love for me as a child
and I long to experience that innocence again.
You come out to meet me on the road
and, to my delight, you do not judge me

or blame me.
You warmly welcome me.
Your great joy, love and care
move me to tears
as you wrap your arms around me.
You have clothed me anew,
fed me with food of all kinds and now
you offer me true Rest.
This kind of Rest in your presence, in your House,
is what my soul has always longed for,
Your loving acceptance encourages me to pray to you
and to be at home with others.
Because you have forgiven me,
I am finding it easier to begin to forgive others
who have offended me.
I am beginning to be more grateful now
for the goodness of others.
My addiction in the past somehow clouded my life and left me
unappreciative of love and kindness coming from others.
I now have resolved to make amends
to those I have hurt in the past.
Lord, give me light each day
so that this new road of love may continue.
Amen.

The Awe of the Childlike

I had time and peace of mind in those days
to watch the busy birds feeding,
hopping about from branch to branch, chirping and alert.
Time to smell the roses and sense the fresh fragrance
of the early summer.
Time to mourn the summer passing
and empathise with the autumn winds,
as they lament and sound the clarion call for winter.
My soul now requires a return, a new visitation,
a new dialogue with the beauty of creation,
so that I might be in touch again; in touch that is with myself,
be present to others and to my Creator.
In that *being really present* we call *prayer*,
surely I will be refreshed, replenished and be recreated, be myself.
Did not the poet Wordsworth say 'the world is too much with us;
late and soon, / getting and spending, we lay waste our powers.
/ Little we see in Nature that is ours / We have given our hearts
away, a sordid boon!'
So we need to return to the garden of our souls.
Do we have the courage to withstand the beauty?
And be silent long enough so that we might hear,
listen and be in touch.

*I wrote this on St Canice's Day, 11 October 2005, after I had
picked up a book, which named some 1,500 Irish saints from the
sixth to eighth century, and looked at the cover depicting a tree
and some small birds.*

The Garden of Your Souls

I wish your soul to be a fruit-bearing garden, where the fruits of the spirit – joy, peace, love, serenity, patience, kindness and self-control will grow in abundance;

Where you will be at one with the true vine, Jesus, the life-giver;

Where you, dear friend, will be a shining pilgrim, a guide example, a signpost and a light to others as to what I can do when you learn to trust in Me and in My care and providence over you, on the journey of life;

Where you will be a channel of true life as you enjoy drinking from the fountain of life, here in my garden of meditation and prayer.

Here you will be an example for all who come thirsting as to where and in whom the soul is satisfied.

I will satisfy souls so that they will not just see and hear the beautiful birds in song but that they will get to sing their own song of songs – they will learn to have their own prayer and poetic love song.

They, indeed, will walk in the light;
will come to Me and find rest.

They will experience my forgiveness and the peace of mind I alone give; they will, indeed, lay down their heavy burdens that have unfairly been put on them by the sin of others and the sin of those who have not shown them that I am the Way, the Truth, and the Life that they seek.

They will get renewed hearts and renewed energy as I bless them in the quiet and in the stillness.

My will is that the young people learn to look at Me, to listen to Me and to pray; that they will stay with Me and be My companions on this hillside, as Patrick, Colmcille and Brigid, their fellow pilgrims, before them.

Here, together, we will learn to rebuild the ancient ruins and build My Kingdom on earth.

'For I will speak to their hearts and their sins I will remember no more.'

Strength in Weakness

In this chapter, I am going to focus on a concept that has two almost contradictory elements to it – the strength, or the power, of weakness and vulnerability.

I remember an occasion, many years ago, when my parents were old and faced the prospect of having to sell a business that had been in the family for four generations. A consultant told them that they were, in fact, in a strong position as they now had a few options from which to choose.

Sometimes this difficulty is what allows a business to expand, diversify, or consider growth in a different direction. If this principle is true in the business world, it is certainly true of the spiritual world. We cry out to God when we are in danger, or when we are afraid of going under. We are like Peter sinking and calling out to Jesus: 'Lord, save me, I perish,' Matthew 14:30-31.

I am going to explore this principle as it has appeared true in my life and the life of the young Columba Community; and you, too, may see this truism as you reflect on your own life.

I chose the title for this chapter because it seems to sum up the theme of my life's experience. As a Christian, and co-builder of the Columba Community, the theme of power or, more accurately, strength in weakness, has emerged over and over again.

As time passed, a profound but simple truth became more and more apparent. That is, that the entire biblical story is one of God's strength and power being manifest in the weaknesses of people who believed in Him, trusted in Him, and waited upon Him.

For a few years after my ordination, it seemed to me that the new life of opportunity to serve the sick, care for parishioners, young and old, be active in visiting homes and making new friends, was very fulfilling. Then the honeymoon period began to wane and, as an older priest said, 'the oils with which you are anointed on the day of ordination begin to dry up.' Life begins to seem like the same old routine.

Youthful sports activity was slowly coming to an end, and loneliness began to set in. Because prayer was being *said*, but not really felt as effective and uplifting, I recall questioning not so much the doctrine of the church, but the lifestyle I was involved in.

This was about seven years after ordination. It was the first time I really questioned the rule of compulsory celibacy for priests, as I started to experience a kind of loneliness amid the business of my daily duties. In the late sixties, there was a lot of talk about the need to be closer involved with people and to become more 'human' as secular priests. Yet, the affective side of life which a good marriage promotes was denied; some would say, 'starved'.

That, together with the fact that serious trouble had broken out in Northern Ireland, gave me a sense of powerlessness and of being somewhat at a distance from reality. It was the nearest thing I have ever felt to depression, when other people described that state to me later. I also felt guilt for such feelings, and wondered what life held in store.

At this point, I went for a one-day retreat to Craighead Retreat Centre, near the town of Hamilton, to listen to a young Jesuit giving a couple of talks, have an opportunity for some quiet time, and to attend Confession – or celebrate The Sacrament of Reconciliation, as they were beginning to call it then.

The priest preached a sermon that I remember to this day. He said: 'All of us have been to Catholic schools and been brought up in Catholic homes. There, we were taught that our good deeds are rewarded and our bad deeds punished. God was somehow a remote figure who watched us from a distance. He was seen as a mathematician, who counted our sins and our virtuous deeds. If we did more good than bad, then we went to Heaven. If not, then we earned Hell or Purgatory.'

He went on to say: 'Nothing could be further from the truth than this if we believe in Jesus Christ, the anointed saviour. We simply do not earn salvation. It is a pure gift from God. All we do is be open to it. We simply accept God's Mercy and say "yes" to it.'

As Paul tells us, 'Where sin abounds, grace does more abound' and 'where we are weakest, there we are strongest.' He said that the blood of Christ is poured forth over our sins and that sins repented of are no problem to God. In this he quoted Martin Luther, who, in turn, emphasised the teaching of Paul in Ephesians 2:8–9. This text tells us that we are saved, not by our own good deeds, but by Christ's good deed on Calvary: 'I repeat, it is owing to his favour that salvation is yours through faith. Neither is it a reward for anything you have accomplished, so let no one pride himself on it. We are truly his handiwork, created in Jesus Christ to lead the life of good deeds which God prepared for us in advance.'

We are saved by grace – God's help, through faith. Faith, here, means trust in that help from God. This may seem very simple and self-evident to the average Christian reader, but to me, at that time, it was an eye-opener. I felt uplifted.

I tend to think in imagery, so as the priest spoke I imagined my life as drawn out on a line from left to right. The line became like a graphic outline of an irregular heartbeat, with parts of it peaking and other parts dipping, or leaving divides. The good news was that the dips, or low times, were not going to damn me after all, but were the very places in which the cross of Christ would sit and allow the blood of Christ to flow over my sin, so that this area would give more glory to God than any other area of my good deeds.

If Jesus' love and merciful forgiveness over my sin gave far more glory to God than my own good deeds, then I am not my own saviour after all. That is cause for great rejoicing. It certainly lifts any sense of stress of having to strive on one's own power. It avoids presumption also, as my own good deeds are more likely to increase in response to being loved this way, or becoming aware of being loved with such mercy and forgiveness. So I thought, perhaps, this is what some evangelicals called the awareness of being saved. This thinking certainly took the grimness and stress out of following the way of Christ.

The young Jesuit went on to tell a story. There is no better way of teasing out a spiritual principle than to illustrate it by an example in a person's life, or attitude. He talked about St Bonaventure, the highly-organised successor of St Francis.

In his lifetime, St Bonaventure founded and built a great number of Franciscan monasteries. As he was dying, after a lifetime of great work, he was visited by a young monk who wanted to console and encourage him. The young novice said: 'Brother Bonaventure, you are very old and will soon die. However, you have nothing to fear. You have done such great work. All you have to do is to hold up to God all the good you have done and you will be welcomed into Heaven.'

The old monk was very weak. He spoke very faintly, while mustering up enough energy just to shake his finger gently at the young monk. He said: 'No. No. As I die, I am holding up to God all my sins, faults and weaknesses. These cry out to God for mercy and forgiveness. For this, I am confident, as the blood of Jesus, my Saviour, washes me clean. This is why I die happy and with great peace.'

A few years ago, prior to the term 'New Evangelisation' being introduced, a survey was carried out among practising Catholic students at third-level college in America. They were asked to imagine God saying to them: 'Give me one good reason why you should get to Heaven?' and to briefly give their answer.

Well, true to form, a few gave the answer mentioned in this chapter. Some spoke of their church attendance and others spoke about their works of charity. Few, if any, pointed to Paul's teaching in Ephesians 2:9: 'it is owing to his favour that salvation is yours through faith. This is not your own doing; it is God's gift'.

There is a line in a Leonard Cohen song which refers to human beings as being flawed or cracked pots. Jeremiah also uses this theme as he watches the potter reshaping the flawed pot with his sensitive hands, until the pot turns out right. However, Cohen says that we need to believe that the cracks are where the light comes in.

The principle of finding strength in weakness applies in many areas of life. Difficult times and trials can be times of opportunity for new initiatives that would never have happened if all of life were to run smoothly. In my own life, and that of the Columba Community, we have seen this truth illustrated again and again.

During my time of 'waiting' after leaving the Cathedral, I got to know both my parents and family members much better than at any other time in my life, perhaps because they understood my vulnerability. I learned to do with little, and to do with plenty, and to depend on God, literally, for the next bite to eat.

This reminds me of the night I was driving along a country road, questioning the Lord about survival, when I suddenly hit a rabbit with the front wheel. I reversed, and found the rabbit half dead. While St Francis may have prayed for its recovery, I 'cuffed it', as we used to do as children in the country, and put it in the boot of the car. The next day, I had roast rabbit with a friend who joined me for lunch and laughter. God provides!

One obvious example of strength and weakness, clear to those who have watched our development over the past thirty-five years, is how I came from not having an official job description in the Derry Diocese to now having, through the Columba Community, five centres, with thirty-five employees, recognised in the Derry Diocesan directory as part of the diocesan set up.

It was always essential for me to have a reference from my home Diocese of Motherwell, during the years of official non-recognition in the Derry–Donegal area. But, apart from having a letter from that diocese every so often, stating that I was 'a reputable priest of the Motherwell Diocese with full faculties in this diocese', I had no income from any official source. Yet, this allowed God the opportunity to provide for the needs we had, and that proved to be such an exciting and life-giving venture, if also challenging.

The struggle that comes from questioning the system, and surviving the difficulties of not being accepted locally for some years, in a way, threw me back on my knees and to listening to what the Lord had in mind. Each time we returned to pray and listen, we got encouragement to keep going.

At one time, this encouragement would come from one of my visits to Cardinal O'Fiaich, or from a fellow priest. At another time, it came from the Spirit in the silence, or from a Scripture reading given by a friend, or member of the community of prayer.

Speaking at the twenty-fifth anniversary of my ordination, which was held in St Columba's, Long Tower, in Derry, Fr Michael Collins noted that I was, at once, enjoying the freedom to follow the direction of the Holy Spirit, but also suffering from not having the full support of the institution locally. He compared my position to having no overcoat to give comfort against the cold.

And yet the freedom, without the awkward overcoat, to do things and to move faster, had its great benefits. It meant that one always had to reflect on the pros and cons of each decision in a deeper way than would be required if one were merely responding to the demands in running a traditional parish and had diocesan appointment.

Times of trial and suffering

I do not want to dwell in depth on the times of trial and suffering I experienced after the unexpected end to my ministry in Derry. The fact is, I am grateful to God for taking care of me, and for all the love and friendship I have experienced over the years. I have learned to forgive those whose actions led to my departure and all the dark days that followed.

However, if it were not for the fact that I was given the Word so strongly and frequently to 'wait on the Lord and have strength renewed', to trust the Lord, 'to mount up on wings as eagles, run and not grow weary, walk and not faint', I would have walked away from the priesthood, and maybe even the Church at that time. God's Word made all the difference.

All of us fall short and, today, if we are to learn anything from the experiences of our institutional church systems, it is that we should never again put our clergy on lonely pedestals. That was an unhealthy position for all of us.

I was sorely tested on many occasions as I tried to pick up the pieces, and continue my priestly ministry as I felt led by the Holy Spirit. One such occasion was in 1990, when Limerick was celebrating an anniversary of its siege.

It seemed right to Fr Damien Ryan and his charismatic prayer committee to invite two Derry charismatic Catholics to speak at their Diocesan Charismatic Conference. Columba Community member, Marguerite Hamilton, was to speak of our common history, with Derry being the only other walled city in Ireland, while I was asked to speak on reconciliation in our land today.

We read about the forthcoming conference in *The New Creation*, a monthly journal issued from the Charismatic Services Committee in Dublin. All preparations and advertisements were in order when, out of the blue, I received a telephone call from Fr Damien. Our speaking engagement had been cancelled. After some questioning, it transpired that Bishop Newman, then the Bishop of Limerick, had contacted Derry and was told that I had nothing to do with the Diocese of Derry and 'had no faculties'.

This kind of thing had happened before, in 1979, when a retreat I was to give in a Newry convent had been called off. When it happened again in 1990, my reaction was to get an update of my letter from Scotland stating that I, indeed, did have faculties. Faculties from a diocese confirm clearly that the priest is in good standing and has permission from his home diocese to preach, offer Mass, and administer sacraments.

The strange thing about this is that, some seventeen years later, I did speak at the Limerick Diocesan weekend conference. In the opening talk, I told the story of the baseball player in the movie, *The Natural*.

Robert Redford played the lead role in the film, a young athlete of seventeen years of age, who was a brilliant baseball player. He got a trial with a famous team in the east in the 1940s, but on the way there he was shot in the side at a hotel where he had stayed the night. He wandered around for years but finally turned up for a trial at the club. He was then thirty-five years of age, and he exposed corruption in the club among players who were fixing the game for monetary gain. Redford played the game of his life, and literally knocked the lights out with one great hit. The movie finished with fireworks and celebrations.

I prayed that our conference in Limerick, at which I was the keynote speaker, albeit seventeen years late, would bring light and hope. I know that the story was not lost on those who were still around the prayer group scene for all those years.

It is difficult to express the level of pain and struggle that went on in those early days, as so much has changed since. Yet I believe it is important not to pretend that life is without struggle. Whose life is?

I recall, especially on Saturday mornings, often sitting on the floor of my bedroom looking up at the mountain outside, and trying to pray. I would have visited the prison prayer meetings on the previous day and got home from Long Kesh late on the Friday night. For some reason, the headaches I suffered from in those days often became more acute on a Saturday morning. These may have been caused partially by ulcers or sinus problems, but I later found out that they were caused mostly by sheer stress. The headache was always on the left side of my head. This side is supposed to be the side of rational thinking, while the right part of the brain is where we get our artistic and intuitive dimensions. I suppose to me, at times, my position did not make rational sense, and not having been given any reason for my being sent back to Scotland, certainly did not make sense to me.

Only in the faith walk could I foresee any merit in this, at times, quite lonely journey. Some relief would come when I could weep on those Saturday mornings. When in prayer, a sense of peace and purpose emerged and then I got the courage to keep going. I cannot underestimate the help and loving support of a few great friends during those years.

After some years of suffering these headaches, a good friend made an appointment for me with a specialist. After a thorough examination in The Royal Hospital, Belfast, the consultant and I had a good talk. He showed me all the test results and, thank God, they were clear. Then he said something from his long experience in this field of medicine. He asked me what the relationship with my boss was like. When I told him about my situation locally, he suggested that I look there for the reason for my headaches. His analysis was pretty accurate as I have not had these headaches since being officially recognised locally.

Having said that, I am also very aware now of the long hours spent praying with sick people, and the intense work that went into making sure that this new work would not fail due to our lack of input, even while we were sure it was guided by God's Holy Spirit.

As I write down these memories, I recall the dire financial constraints of those days of the late seventies and mid-eighties. Money for heating oil simply was not there. So I found myself praying and reading in my bedroom, comfortably wrapped up in a blanket, as this was the only warm place in the house.

Few people appreciated the meagre resources we had to keep going, and how we had to cost every meal, telephone call, and trip with the old van to Derry when we lived at St Anthony's in the mid-eighties. What we were led into by experience in an existential way, we later would read about in the spirituality of St Ignatius, which we used to help lead retreats at St Anthony's Retreat Centre.

Some of the principles of Ignatian spirituality are worth recording here, as they relate to this theme of what real strength is, and what the wrong use of power can reap by way of devastation spiritually.

The mentality promoted by Jesus in his charter for Christian living, in *The Beatitudes*, is surely what we require to aspire to as a people who call ourselves Christian. The Sermon on the Mount begins by stating: 'Blessed are the poor in spirit.' The poor in spirit are those who really know they are reliant on God. They need God.

The principle of new opportunity that is often available in times of trial or difficulty is well known. It is exemplified, first of all by Jesus in his early hidden life, and especially by his Passion and cross. He is wounded by those he came to help. He is rejected by his own people, and by all of us who do not welcome him in the poor and sick, and those wounded by society.

Is it any wonder then that Paul, in his Letter to the Hebrews, invites us, who say we are followers, to 'Go with him outside the walls', identify with the marginalised Christ, and have the courage to stand for his teaching in difficult times, or in times of persecution.

Just as Jesus, at times, questioned the will of the Father and then moved in His ways, so we too need to choose His ways, even when unpopular or at risk of being misunderstood or judged by the world. It all depends on how we are led by His Spirit.

If we are to look at the story of Paul, we see that his conversion to truth entailed a time when he was struck down from his haughty position as a self-righteous persecutor of Christians. He was struck blind. He was then led by the hand for healing and instruction to Simon, one of those he had set out to persecute. This sense of weakness, or need to rely on a Christian like Simon, was part of Paul's journey in finding strength through weakness.

Similar stories can be recorded throughout Christendom. St Francis came to belief and conversion after being struck down with shock and shattered after his experience of violence and war. St Ignatius, also, was wounded after a battle as a soldier. In his time of convalescence, he was led to follow Christ and founded the Jesuits. These examples of men, who were graced by God to make a choice for good and to follow Christ, are ideal examples of the options we have before us on our daily journey through life.

Exercises of St Ignatius
In the exercises of St Ignatius, we are told that the basic structure of temptation to sin involves our attraction to Wealth (having),

Honour (appearing) and Pride (being able). These all come from the spirit of evil in us and around us. The grace we get to overcome these involves the Spirit of Good, which allows us, like St Francis, to choose the Christian virtues of Poverty (being held), Belittlement (being subject) and Humility (being possessed by Christ).

Wealth versus poverty of spirit

By wealth we mean an obsessive preoccupation for the world of having, whether it is material, intellectual, temperamental or spiritual. The lust for possession dominates my whole existence and becomes its driving force. This, of course, includes the possession of others, which is the greatest of the sins of wealth. The root of this is wanting deep self sufficiency, in which we bolster ourselves up by possessions, despising or undervaluing the contribution of others and even, eventually, God's grace.

This is the most fundamental temptation, and we saw it in evidence in a big way during the time of the boom, or, more accurately, bloated Celtic Tiger years, in Ireland. Here, misuse of authority occurred in economic and state leadership; often this temptation was at the root of it.

Whereas, when we are poor, we realise that we are needy and resort to others, and especially to Our Lord, for help. Poverty of spirit may or may not involve actual material poverty, but it certainly does involve a special mentality, whereby the person accepts that they are being held in all aspects of life, without hanging onto any areas of life for themselves alone. It involves consciously placing myself in the hands of others so that they can make good use of my gifts. For Ignatius, this is the virtue that generates all others, and without which it is impossible to build a spiritual life on truth.

Honour versus belittlement

By honour, here, we mean an obsessive preoccupation with the world of 'appearances' (institutional, social, intellectual, spiritual) which would lead to vain glory – a subtle temptation, often based on glory in things achieved which were not God's will. In our hedonistic society, honour is seen as the key to worldly success.

Belittlement, on the other hand, is accepting being 'subject' to God's will. It is best practiced by imitation of Christ. It does not mean a false humility that would lead to gross undervaluing of self, but it prevents an overvaluing of self, or a sense that I do not owe all the glory to God for any gift used and developed.

Pride versus humility:

Pride, as we see it in the story of the fallen angels, or the story of Adam and Eve, is when we aim to take God's place and dominate others and situations for our own selfish advantage. When we see the Father as the Principal of life, as Jesus does, and we also take the role of servant and act for the betterment of others, then we grow in this spirit of humility. When I become gift to others, I have then begun to share in the Lord's experience. Then I will have become a true Christian who brings a joy no one can take away.

Gethsemane

Jesus in His place of vigil prayer – the garden.

Not for the first time is Jesus praying, searching for the way to react and asking the Father to reveal His will. He is saying:

Father, You know I love You and I trust You.

In my human nature, I do not want to suffer, please take this cross, this trial, this burden of impending humiliation and hurtful time away from me.

I do not want to die.

I would much rather go on healing the sick, giving the lepers and the alienated new dignity and consoling, with Your words and deeds of compassion, the widows, the orphans.

I want to convert the tax collectors so that they become happy givers to the poor and needy.

I, in My own will, would like to stay with these apostles who are sleeping here and wake them up, teach them more about You, My Father and their Father, and form more and more apostles.

Being in an agony, He prayed the longer and, after being crushed in His humanity, He learned to sense the hidden presence of the Father. Then the Lord prayed again:

But not My will – let Your will be done.

I surrender to You My will, even though the sense I have in My listening to Your voice is that You are asking Me to lay down My life for the world of Your people.

You want Me to be the sacrificial lamb of the new covenant so that all who will get to believe in Me and in Your plan for them, will experience a spiritual awakening and have life that will be like an everlasting spring of Love.

I will do it, because though I am terrified and sweating blood, I know I can trust You and You will somehow give more life to the world by My obedient giving.

You will send Your spirit to teach through My followers,

You will continue to heal spirits and emotions, and often bodies of many millions through those who will believe in Me.

Therefore I say I do. Your ways, not My ways be done.

Then the angels came and ministered to Him. He received courage. For thousands of years to come others would benefit and receive grace.

~

Are We a People of Hope?

Crucified, Jesus, You were laid in the arms of your mother.
If hope in You is victory in defeat, then love is the new strength
we get through death.
Jesus, as You walked on Your way to Calvary You saw
confusion, pain and also hatred, fear and greed, in the faces of
the crowd.
You were in the thick of the great spiritual battle between good
and evil and in your absorbing of all the pain and evil, You offer
to take out the poison of greed, domination and violence, from
the heart of fallen humanity.
You remain silent before the lies of your accusers.
On the cross, You got the Father's help and said, 'forgive them,
they know not what they do'.
In Your apparent defeat You score the greatest victory of all. You
surrender to the Father of love.
You let go of your loving mother, your faithful friends like John
and Mary, who stood by the cross with your mother.
You were driven outside the walls – thus You identify with
everyone who feels cut off.
You, though innocent, became the bearer of sin and loneliness.
You suffered all the effects of our sin indeed, as Paul, your
chosen disciple would put it, You 'became sin'.
You became so ugly with the effects of sin that people, Isaiah
tells us, would turn away from You and could not even bear to
look at You.

Yet, You managed to say 'into Your hands I commit My spirit'.
You said to those at the foot of the cross, 'mother, behold thy
son and son, behold thy mother'.
And finally, Your last words, 'it is finished'.
Your human sacrifice to the Father is complete.
Teach me, like You, to lean into the time and places of pain, as
by taking up my cross I know You will make it light.
Help me not to run away from the challenge,
but to bear it patiently.
Teach me to sit before You and just know your ways
will lead to new life.
To hope in You, God, is the most Christian act we can do
because it means recognising that You can never fail us,
however painful or pitiful the circumstances.
Are we a people of hope?

The Cross

You marked my days like an icon,
a stamp, a seal upon my life.
You are the unwelcome guest,
who yet demands a welcome.
You stand aloof to challenge us to surrender.
Yet, you will be a bridge to new horizons,
if we but embrace you;
even grow to love you
as I love the One who died
on you – for me – outside the city.
For it is He I welcome and embrace.
It is He who has given meaning to my emptiness
and healing to my wounded heart.
Amen.

Seek First the Kingdom of God

When I felt undervalued, I came to you
And in your smile you said,
'You think you are not appreciated.'
It was then, as I looked at your knowing gaze,
it dawned how little was my suffering
and sense of loss compared to yours.
Yet, you trusted that Your Father would raise
You up and that real eternal good
would come from your offering of love.
And You say to us who turn to You,
'I appreciate You.
My Father rejoices in you, so beloved, be happy always.
Continue to run the good race.
Continue to fight the good fight
and you will never grow weary of doing good because,
I am with you.'

Whether it is the quest for the holy grail or
the search for the pearl of great price,
each of us is searching for happiness.
There is a heart-shaped hole at the centre of all of us
that only our union with God can fill.
How we attempt to satisfy that central need for love
will depend on what we think will give the ultimate happiness.
For one person, it may be the quest for riches at all costs,

for another, it may be looking for the perfect partner
or the perfect relationship.
For Solomon, it was the gift of wisdom,
that union with the greater power
that would help him to make
the right decisions for all his people
and God recommended that.

Today, we are called to review our priorities,
to seek first the Kingdom of God.
It begins with a listening to our own heart and God's call to us
to love him above all and then,
to learn from Him how to love others.
How do I listen?
How do I learn to pray with the heart?
I need to begin to raise my own heart to Him,
my own wounded heart, my own healed heart,
my own disappointed heart, my own broken heart,
to come, just as I am, and be before Him and His compassion.
His loving heart will, if I go before him and be still,
connect with my life
and begin to teach me how again to rebuild.
He will give me wisdom.
He will give me peace.
He will lighten up my path and give me His word of wisdom,
as He did to Solomon,
so that I do the right thing.
Let my prayer be that of Solomon,
to discern between good and evil,
this is worth more than silver or gold.

The secret is in giving it all away.
Like St Francis,

we receive as we give.
We need first to be humble and searching before God.
Jesus, You stand outside and wait for the invitation
to fill us with Your being, to live in us.
Pearl of great price,
am I ready to give up all else?
The Lord is sad when He sees otherwise,
a possible great opportunity missed,
we choose death rather than life.
But, when we choose life
then God will reward us one hundred fold!

Twelve Steps Model for Church Renewal

The twelve-step programme for recovery from everything from slavery to drugs, alcohol and gambling has become a model for people all over the world who wish to deal with their addictions and problems. It is based on a simple message from the Bible where the sufferer realises, often after much pain, that he or she cannot go on alone.

They cry out to God, or the higher power, to save them from insanity and destruction. Gradually, and daily, with the help of the fellowship members, they get to hand their lives over to the god of their understanding. They get help from a sponsor to make an inventory of their hurts, resentments and failings (sins), and find another person they can confess these character defects to. They also get advice on how and when to make restitution, and work at making amends in a way that is feasible.

Over the years working with alcoholics in recovery, I have witnessed the power of God's grace at work. My contention is that there is no sense in convicting people without also convincing them that there is hope.

For those who profess the Christian faith, it means introducing them to the forgiveness of God in Jesus Christ. This is not to take God for granted, but to experience being loved in a way that we should never want to leave His home again. It means praying that the embrace experienced by the Prodigal Son be the experience of each of us who decide to go back to the Father's house.

Where sin abounds, grace does more abound. At the risk of being accused of over emphasising the importance of the Twelve

Steps, let me repeat that the first step is to admit that I am powerless over this addiction. It is as simple as that. I cannot handle it. I have tried everything, and I now know I cannot stay sober through my own power.

The second step is to acknowledge that I have come to believe, from listening to other people, that a power greater than myself could help me in this situation, and could save me from insanity.

The same principles of the Twelve Steps are in the spiritual exercises of St Ignatius. The central teaching in these spiritualities asks us to have an attitude of constant repentance, prayer of listening, and awareness of God's nearness.

Having worked with recovering alcoholics, drug addicts and gamblers, it has often occurred to me that the Twelve Steps are the principle ways to holiness advocated by both the Old and New Testaments.

The Alcoholics Anonymous programme has been promoted since 1936 when Bill W, Dr Bob, and a few others started reading extracts from the New Testament and helped each other understand their compulsive natures and addiction to alcohol. In their quest to get practical help to remain sober and content, they focused especially on the letters of Paul to the Corinthians (Chapter 13), the Letter of St James and the Sermon on the Mount. Their faith in God, 'The Higher Power', grew.

They were also influenced by the Oxford Group, which, not unlike any Bible-based prayer group, emphasised the Lordship of Christ and the experience of being renewed in the Holy Spirit.

I believe it is impossible to have a contented and prolonged recovery from any addiction without growth in faith and real trust in the God of our understanding. It seems that faith in a higher power has strengthened resolve and aided sobriety.

Expressed in language that would appeal to the religious and non-religious alike, the twelve-step programme has worked for millions of people with all kinds of addictions, human weaknesses, sins and problems. It is now recognised as the most successful way of not only coping with addictions, but of doing so in a way that brings contentment.

Through our own power, and with our own self-will, we may, for a time, abstain from alcohol or other substance abuse, but we can become a 'dry drunk', and, without the spiritual help and ongoing structure that the Twelve Steps bring, we do not enjoy contented sobriety.

Surely there are lessons of hope in this Biblically-based programme for the Irish Church today, and for all of us who seek a way forward. There are lessons here, in particular, for the hierarchy and for clergy whose ministry has been undermined by the child abuse scandal and by misuse of power.

People generally are surprised to learn that much of what happens in a centre treating addiction has more to do with correcting 'stinking thinking', as they say in AA circles, than it has to do with just stopping drinking, or quitting the addictive behaviour.

The fourth and fifth steps of the AA programme have much to teach us in church leadership circles. They speak of 'making a general inventory of our lives and finding one other person in whom we can confide the nature of our character defaults', and of 'making amends to those we have hurt, except where doing so would cause further injury or hurt'.

The sin of the abuse of children by any adult is horrific and soul destroying. It cries to Heaven and to the God of Justice for repentance and healing. It echoes from the corridors of industrial schools in Ireland to the four shores of the nation and beyond.

Worldwide statistics say that a considerable percentage of women with alcohol problems have been sexually abused as children. Indeed, the effects of this degradation of human dignity are such that addiction counsellors refer such clients for intense, prolonged aftercare counselling to a specialist rape and incest counsellor. This service is essential if contented sobriety is to happen and have any chance of continuing. Indeed, the other forms of abuse, such as neglect, criticism or physical abuse need to be also held out for healing if the childhood wounds that often lead to addiction are to be dealt with.

Once, I was praying for a child of nine or ten years of age who had been sexually abused by a priest who had begun his prison sentence by that time. The child, hiding behind her mother, was at first sobbing quietly. As we prayed, the sobbing turned into bawling that could only be described as the broken-hearted wail of an adult in the body of a little girl. It was a clear example to me of where prayer for deliverance from evil is required in pastoral ministry.

This child received professional and spiritual help, and today seems to have recovered from, or survived, that terrible trauma. Many victims of abuse never get treatment or even get to talk about their pain and trauma.

When the twelve-step programme works, the person is no longer feeling the powerful compulsion to drink, but he or she is mindful of always being an alcoholic. Like St Paul, they realise that the power of God is manifest in their weakness and they realise the real need for God's power in their lives each day, as they live one day at a time. If, as a church, we are to govern with this kind of humility, and recognise our past habits of misusing power and authority, then a spiritual programme like the Twelve Steps may help.

Perhaps, as I heard someone suggest, we need to pray and hope that the abused will invite us to come and listen to them. We need to pray that, if and when that day comes, we are spiritually ready to know how to come alongside the victims and know how to reverence them. Then we will know the privilege of having our own dignity restored.

These wounded people can give us, the clergy, back our unique vocation and position of trust. They can give us what the recovering alcoholic gives those privileged to listen to his or her story about renewed faith in God and humanity. Having someone tell you humbly about their failings and hurts during their past lives is a rare and blessed privilege. To see such people walk free of the heavy burden of the past and walk each day the walk of serenity, is one of the joys in ministry that is difficult to surpass.

It would be my dream that each priest, saddened by the reports of abuse of the innocent in recent years, would have the privilege of helping to release the captive and undo the evil. To watch our higher power, Jesus our Redeemer, restore the life of a child is surely comparable to the experience of Peter as he watched Jesus restore the daughter of Jairus to life.

What a great day it would be if the daughter, sulking and enraged by abuse, or the son, seething with false guilt and unresolved anger, were to be set free. What a time of liberty would be declared in Ireland. Then, many would again experience rebirth in the spirit, a sense of cleansing, joy and forgiveness, and a real sense of being washed in the blood of the Lamb. The innocent, vindicated children of God would be set free.

Perhaps, the exposure of clerical sins in this area is but the Lord's way of beginning to call the entire population to account. Unquestionably, this problem needs addressed throughout our society, as do other injustices and offences against the innocent.

Any real and honest effort to address the clerical child abuse issue by Church leadership would not alone require admission of neglect, denial, culpable ignorance and genuine repentance, but would need to include a sincere purpose of amendment as well.

Again, to learn from the AA programme for recovery, we could look at 'people, places and things' associated with the addiction. In other words, to use the Church's phrase on this, we need to sincerely reflect on the 'occasions of sin' and the circumstances that enabled clerical child abuse to develop relatively unchallenged.

Recent figures show that recruits to the seminary are older. Whatever their age group, let us hope that they be encouraged to pray and to minister with the power to heal. I often wonder why so few priests pray for healing with the wounded and sick by the laying on of hands, despite what we see in the life of Jesus himself, especially as portrayed in Luke's Gospel, and despite the commissioning that Jesus gives to his followers at the end of Matthew's Gospel: 'Go forth, lay your hands on the sick, and they shall be healed.'

We see the first miracle of Peter after Pentecost is to heal the paralysed man. Peter says: 'Gold and silver I have not, but what I have I will give you. In the name of Jesus Christ arise and walk!' The Acts of the Apostles contain many healing stories also. This ministry of healing is to be expected. After all, Jesus promised this as one of the signs that would go with the genuine teaching of the Gospel. Mark's Gospel (16:20) tells us: 'The eleven went forth and preached everywhere. The Lord continued to work with them throughout and confirm the message through the signs which accompanied them.'

When we, as clergy, are reluctant to pray with the sick for God's healing to come upon them in some sense, the question has to be asked: is there a crisis of faith? Do we really believe in the presence, power and directives of Christ? Often, a crisis of faith precedes a crisis in morals. We certainly have witnessed the latter.

Again, it is a question of recognising our powerlessness and being open to be led to rely on the power of the God given to us in the spirit. This happens when we finally realise we have nowhere else to turn but to the God who is waiting to be gracious to us.

Ongoing Development of the Columba Community

I would like to finish with a note of hope for the future of the Church in Ireland. In doing so, I tell the story of the development of the Columba Community, and trust that many other new communities may spring up, as they did during the Golden Age in Ireland.

On 30 August 1995, before a packed congregation in St Eugene's Cathedral, Bishop Seamus Hegarty officially recognised the Columba Community as a lay institute, or a private association of the faithful. These are canonical terms of new branches of the Church that are defined by the new Canon Law of 1982.

I had known Seamus Hegarty from our student days in St Eunan's Secondary Boarding School in Letterkenny, and had always got on well with him. Ironically, when he was Bishop of Raphoe we had spoken about transferring the entire Columba Community work and model of basic Christian community to the Raphoe Diocese. We had talked about making a retreat centre at Gartan, where Colmcille was born, and developing something like the complex that we have now at the White Oaks Rehabilitation Centre.

On returning to Ireland and, especially after leaving St Eugene's Cathedral in 1978, I often visited Bishop Hegarty in Letterkenny and I remember him saying, on one occasion, that when a new bishop was appointed to Derry he would personally talk to him about accepting me and my work into the Derry Diocese.

As it turned out, he was that new Bishop of Derry and he told me that he had every intention of accepting me and my community into the Derry Diocese officially, and canonically. Providentially, Monsignor Joey Donnelly became parish priest of Iskaheen, our local parish in Co. Donegal. He not only was vicar general but a canon lawyer also, with great knowledge of the Church's recognition of new Christian communities. He was instrumental in facilitating ourselves and Bishop Hegarty to allow for our canonical recognition.

Firstly, I was appointed for a while to assist in the nearby Holy Family Parish in Derry. Bishop Hegarty asked me to help out there, but I still lived in the farmhouse at St Anthony's and served the Columba Community.

While there were indications from both the parish priest and Bishop Hegarty that they would like me to be full-time in the parish, needless to say that had to be discerned against what I have written earlier, and how the Lord was leading me in forming the Columba Community as a basic Christian community.

I told the parish priest there at the time that I would work in the parish as much as I could, but that I had a responsibility to the community that had been with me for seventeen years prior to that. I had to ask myself the question: if I go back to a parish and leave the developing Columba Community, is that saying that God somehow had made a mistake or that I had totally misinterpreted His will for me during the past seventeen years?

Too much had happened, which had given new hope and new life to many people, for me to believe that the continued work of the Columba Community was not my calling.

It would help if we had an alternative governance system for energetic Catholics who want to pray, develop spiritually and serve the larger community in a specific apostolate. This would allow the basic communities to be part of the church, even if not led by the parish priest; ideally, there should be one unit where the talent and aspirations of all parishioners are encouraged.

However, while I would hope to unite both governance systems, my sense is that priests and people need to be convinced if the basic Christian communities are to play their part in the renewal of the Irish Church.

Priests in parishes, by the very nature of the present system, would find it very difficult to develop lay ministry in a meaningful way. In some sense, in my own case, being somewhat disenfranchised turned out to be an advantage in ministry.

I believe that a priest, due to the tradition and structure that he is in, would find it very difficult to build a basic Christian community from the grass roots. It would need to begin in a way similar to how St Francis began: in poverty and without the appointment and recognition that comes from the legal rational authority system that is inherent in Church structures at the moment. This brings up the whole question of the governing system of parishes and, indeed, of dioceses at large.

New procedures

If learning is a change in behaviour as a result of some experience, then the Catholic Church in Ireland has certainly learned a very expensive lesson. Indeed, some report that, by far, the most safety conscious institution in this land is the Church, in its protective measures governing vulnerable adults and children from any possible abuse. This is good to see.

We always need to remember that we are all sinners, and that some of the structures and procedures we followed in the past were faulty and harmful, to say the least. Consequently, the Church in Ireland has suffered a lot of criticism, much of it justified, about the way that it has handled the cases where some clerics have sexually abused young people. The misuse of authority has accompanied the exposure of this problem.

The clear misuse of authority in handling child sexual abuse and dealing with the perpetrators exposes another underlying problem: the use of authority by Church leaders, in general, in a way that leaves people with little or no redress, leaving them powerless, whether they are maltreated as clergy or laity. The victim of such misuse of authority, be he/she cleric, religious or lay person, may turn to God and find there a future ministry – as happened in my own case – or they could become embittered and disillusioned and give up their exercise of faith altogether.

The latter would be to forfeit one's very soul, or spiritual life, to an unworthy authority. It would also be a most immature response to an action taken by another human being, who may misuse authority because of their own immaturity. If so, they need to be prayed for.

We use a phrase at the White Oaks addiction treatment centre when dealing with resentments which can lead the addict back to drinking or drugging. You tell the addict how illogical it is to give one's offender 'free digs in your head'. That means allowing someone to live rent free in your mind! Only the Lord, Christ the anointed One, deserves that position.

The apostolates our Columba Community have become involved in should help illustrate the model of a basic Christian community church. We would say that basic communities need to be part of the renewal of the Irish Church if we are to recognise this time as a time of God's visitation and a great opportunity for Kingdom building, renewal of structures and lay involvement.

A way forward
Both the existing parish model of church and the basic Christian community model need to work in tandem and with respect for

each other as the number of small communities develops. One possible way to facilitate both the traditional ministries in the parish and develop new ones for small basic communities, like our own, would be to begin with sincere and meaningful pastoral councils.

Again, I argue that even prior to that there would need to be, as in the early churches of St Paul, an emphasis on the need for every person who calls themselves Christian to have, in reality, a personal spiritual relationship with Our Lord Jesus Christ and have a love of his Word, so that, as a group, they are led by His Spirit and not just by the strongest or most outspoken personality. I am speaking here about Baptism in the Spirit, which needs to be an ongoing experience.

The members of such a parish pastoral council would meet to pray together each week and be ready to proceed in listening and in doing what is discerned to be the will of God for the people whom they are privileged to serve.

From these groups, men and women would emerge who would become deacons and deaconesses. These would 'serve at tables', to use the term from the Acts of the Apostles. That service could cover all the administrative duties of the present parish priest as well as ministering in other ways, such as teaching and preaching the truths of the faith.

In that type of parish, it would be easy to see how new Christian communities would emerge and be part of the pastoral council. It will require leadership and the fire and power of the Holy Spirit.

I see, in this model, a great help in implementing some of Pope Francis' wishes for the future of the Church ministry.

Consecrated ministries

If evangelisation of our churched people and society at large is such an urgent need – and it is – we need to have this vision

241

fulfilled. Then the concept of a priest as possessing all the charisms, as well as all authority for ministry in the parish, will gradually yield to allow the priesthood of all believers in Christ its rightful position.

Simply put, the good Christian man or woman in the parish who, by God's grace, is a good administrator, for example, could be 'ordained' or, perhaps, consecrated to administer the parish property and finance, with the appropriate safeguards. The good Christian counsellor, with appropriate spiritual formation, could be officially consecrated to do just that, work as a good counsellor, an anam cara, and a good confessor. The teacher of Christian truths and the inspired preacher could each have their ministry recognised and validated locally, just as the special ministers of the Eucharist are presently recognised officially.

I recall many years ago, in Albuquerque, witnessing people coming to my friend Bob Flannigan for spiritual direction. He and his wife, Jean, had been involved in such a ministry for many years.

For the variety of needs there must be a variety of gifts to be called forth, recognised, encouraged and officially appointed. If, traditionally, the term 'ordination' has been used exclusively for the concept of dedicating clergy, then the term 'consecrated' may be the more acceptable one to use.

We, clergy, are generally slow to change our way of thinking and prefer a 'business as usual church', even in the face of becoming ignored as irrelevant. For obvious reasons, those who made it through the seminary and stayed in the ministry over the past thirty or forty years are, by and large, more likely to follow the party line and be reluctant to embrace a change in thinking about ministry.

The divergent and more intuitive type of thinker is less likely to have survived the type of training that we received in 'formation', at the seminaries of the early sixties. Thinking outside the box, or taking a more objective view of priesthood and how that relates to the Church's call to holiness, as described in the Constitution of the Church in the teaching of Vatican II, is certainly required if we are to feed the flock entrusted to us.

Incidentally, I dislike the phrase 'thinking outside the box'; I prefer to think of simply making the box bigger! Who has the right to determine how big this imaginary box should be in the first place?

Radical as it may seem to some, we need to urgently look at empowering people in the use of their talents in ministry, even when this entails re-examining our own role and handing over many of our functions and ministries to the laity. At least, we need to begin to enjoy shared ministry at a wider level with our appreciative brothers and sisters.

It seems to me that we have been talking about lay ministry for fifty years, but little or nothing has changed, even if the need, apart from the right, of our baptised people is clear. As the Simon and Garfunkel song goes, 'we continue to continue'. As long as some are still 'going to Mass' we tend to let the good be the enemy of the best by not spending prime time praying with and encouraging the people in each district who are already called to ministry in the area's mentioned earlier.

Recently, some dedicated lay Catholics, who are part of a parish council, told me that it is that in name only. They feel that it is more like a traditional parish committee, where the priest, conditioned as he is to control, prevents the full and positive contribution of the talented laity. Sadly, this may be true in some cases but surely prayer and mutual respect will allow for positive change.

A new mindset

A few years ago, a priest from a parish in the south of Ireland came to visit me and wondered how he might bring new life into the parish ministry. When I mentioned a pastoral council, he said that he had tried that and it did not work. The trouble was that a few who had been appointed to responsible roles took over and hogged the entire proceedings. They misused their power. I asked him the obvious question: where do you think they learned that way of running a parish?

Personally, I believe that the conversion type experience that often happens via a crisis or a born-again experience is required before we enter into a real fervour and excitement about the gospel.

In sociological terms, the priest and laity who will pave the way for a more inclusive priesthood of all believers exercising ministry, will experience a paradigm shift in thinking about the concept of priesthood.

The priest must be ready to risk losing his present job description and save, or find, his vocation in the process. This will bring a blessing to his fellow pilgrims in the parish, whose salvation and fulfilment in Christian vocation is just as important as the priest's.

He will also face the problem of codependent laity who know no other concept of being Ecclesia. Like the family members of the alcoholic, they have become conditioned to the situation and will find it difficult, at first, to step out and exercise their newfound freedom as privileged members of the priesthood of Jesus Christ. It is so easy for all of us to become institutionalised.

The pastor's true calling, surely, is to animate and strengthen the faith of the people and, as a privileged brother, be simultaneously strengthened and fed by the gifts of his or her fellow pilgrims.

Sadly, however, at clerical conferences and at retreats in the past we were encouraged to fraternise almost exclusively with fellow priests. In fact, there is sometimes the suggestion by implication that the laity are not to be trusted with real levels of responsibility and spiritual ministry. This reflects more on our own failure to evangelise properly and on our consequent insecurity, than on the readiness to serve effectively, and the ability to minister responsibly, that exists in our people throughout the country.

In fairness to the parish priests, however, it must be said that discernment and prayer for such is essential, if we are to call the proper people for various ministries. We need to be aware of the danger of lay 'clerics', who might even unconsciously want to take over the role of controller in parish work. Indeed, there is always a danger of mirror imaging and 'becoming what we dislike the most', to use a phrase from Carl Jung, the eminent Swiss psychologist.

We have seen this in political circles, so in any development of lay ministry in the Church it is important to be aware of the motives of applicants. This danger, however, must not deter us from seeking to develop the Kingdom of God by active sharing of ministry.

When people today are walking away from church attendance, surely part of the reason is because when they were attending they were not called on to make a difference. They have not experienced being respected, encouraged or empowered to be fellow servants and evangelists in their own parish.

An example of this is a visit I had by a couple of Jehovah Witnesses, who were enthusiastically promoting Scripture. As ex-Catholics, they talked about never being challenged to really study the Word of God or to evangelise when they were 'active' Catholics.

In calling the laity to serve and develop their gifts, the priest himself will find affirmation and help in his own special calling and giftedness. He will grow with the spirit of discernment and continue to build the kingdom with others. So he will grow in enthusiasm about the entire concept of shared spiritual ministry with his brothers and sisters in the parish. Then it will not seem to him to be a mere power shift in a secular institute.

If his concept of job description is that of a spiritual leader and not a manager in charge of the plant, then initiatives for real change are likely to come from such a cleric. He will be a leader of real change and enjoy his vocation.

The thirst for Christian community

When I was working in the Cathedral parish in Derry back in the seventies, I prayed that one day I would be part of a lay basic Christian community, that would be centred on prayer and be led into appropriate apostolates. That prayer has been answered and, while the journey has not been without some pain and suffering, great things have happened.

As a small group of fourteen people, who have met at least weekly – some of us almost daily – over the past thirty years, we have witnessed God's grace at work in many people's lives and we have been guided to start many good works.

It seems significant to say that these works and, more importantly, the good people whose good work and prayer brought them into being, came in times of desperation when people needed such places.

Equally so, there is a great thirst and hunger for spiritual experience in Ireland today. People have had a glut of television and the materialistic lifestyle that has been challenged by the recent economic downturn. Even if the economy improves, people may now accept that the heart-shaped hole at the centre of our being can only be filled by God, and the things of the Spirit.

My memory returns to praying during the hunger strike in Columba House and offering Mass with a group of prisoners' relatives. It was midsummer and as we prayed with the window open the smell of smoke from a nearby burnt out vehicle was in the air. A different kind of incense, you may say, but a stark reminder of how desperately and seriously we required the power only God could give.

Then we received the guidance that the Holy Spirit is free to give. Guidance prevailed as we shared God's word joyfully, especially at that time when the answers were not forthcoming from the institutions of church and state. We were guided as a small group to 'wait upon the Lord' (Isaiah 40:31). So, we persevered, without much official support, and enjoyed the journey as well as the longed for destination.

In addition to weekly visits to Long Kesh Prison, also known as the Maze, and some of our female members visiting the women in Armagh jail occasionally, the Community responded to an ecumenical need. For six years, on the first Sunday of the month, we held 'Christians Together' meetings.

I list the works we were led into to make a point, which is central to any genuine basic community, that is, we are not to be a cosy huddle of the like-minded or group of praying people, comforting and strengthening as that may be. We need to be always reaching out to the poor or deprived, materially and spiritually, if we are to fit the criteria of Christian community.

Praying for charismatic gifts
In the Columba Community, we believe in the charismatic gifts as spoken of by St Paul in Corinthians. The Charismatic movement in the late sixties and early seventies throughout the Catholic Church was of God and, for me, it was what gave life and direction to the documents of Vatican II. Indeed, the new experience of the Holy Spirit in the Charismatic movement allowed the Word of God to be a real lamp for our feet and a light for our eyes.

Sometimes, we presuppose a faith that simply is not there, and the charismatic prayer meetings were what brought the faith to life for many people. Sadly, many in leadership in the Church did not take the opportunity to get involved.

My prayer is that we will all begin to listen to God's Word in prayer and share in small groups and then see where we are led. Building new models of basic Christian community in Ireland, and in the western church generally, is possible. This will complement the larger parish structure and not contradict it.

It will require a major shift in thinking, both by clergy and laity alike, as we have been conditioned to the present set up long before we had an educated laity. It will require us all to be more focused on a model of authority that emphasises service rather than control. It will require patience to unlearn some habits.

We can begin by prayer and reflection on the life of Jesus in John's Gospel, for example. It will take time. It will not happen overnight. I am reminded of a statement by Revd Joe Petree, a Methodist minister from North Carolina, when he spoke to the Columba Community years ago: 'Start somewhere, doing something. The Lord can't change the direction of a mule that ain't moving!'

It is my vision and hope that small communities will sprout up all over Ireland, like small springs, to again irrigate this holy land of ancient saints and scholars. Indeed, each area could look at the charism of its local native saint and see if there are gifts there to be resurrected, or imitated. We need to have fresh wineskins, fresh new governance systems, to contain the fresh wine the Spirit of God is always pouring out for us to avail of and enjoy.

Finally, I will outline what, for me, have been the four main foundation stones of our community, which have enabled it to achieve good things and, please God, will allow it to develop further in facilitating God's Kingdom.

These are what Fr Francis Martin once spoke of as the marks of the 'Normal Christian Life'. They are Prayer, Community Membership, Evangelisation and Reconciliation with Repentance. I have teased these out throughout this book. I trust the reader will also see the simplicity and the clarity of these four essential elements in building God's Kingdom on earth.

The normal Christian life
Prayer: The raising up of the mind and heart to God. It is surely central if we are to practice our faith and worship God. It is to be like the branch Jesus speaks of when he asks us to be at one with him, the vine. We cannot be alive spiritually without it, as prayer is the meeting place with God. Listening prayer is where we get our guidance and inspiration.

Community
We need to belong and be at one with others. To illustrate again from nature, we are like logs in good formation in the fire. We thus give warmth and light as we glow and grow together. If one log is removed, the fire in it soon loses its flame and dies out. We belong together, with Christ at the centre. We define Christian community, therefore, as 'a network of interpersonal relationships based on our primary relationship with Jesus as Lord and Saviour'.

Evangelisation
This takes place when, like the early Christians, we love one another. It is what happened when our Celtic saints went to the continent. They lived the monastic life and drew people to Christ by their lifestyle and dynamic faith. Again, the image of the burning logs in perfect formation comes to mind. They produce heat, warmth and light. We offer wisdom and the sense that we

have found the Messiah/Lord/Saviour when we have the worthwhile good news to offer.

Reconciliation and Repentance

Any Christian community must desire reconciliation with all the other communities in Christ's body, the Church. That is true of the communities within the Catholic parish or area. It is true also for our honest sharing with reformed traditions. As there are other sheep that are not of this fold, we need to pray and work for the unity Jesus prays for. Remember also Jesus' last prayer for us, his disciples, was to ask the Father that He may be in us and we may be one. 'Father, may they be one in us, so that the love with which you loved me may be in them, and so that I may be in them' (John 17:26).

This is the goal of Christ's desire for us. May you and I allow his prayer to be answered and may He live in us always.

A Homily

Given by Bishop Seamus Hegarty on the occasion of the Canonical Recognition of the Columba Community at St Eugene's Cathedral, Derry, on 31 August 1995.

This evening we celebrate a votive Mass of the Holy Spirit. In this Eucharistic celebration – since Eucharist means giving thanks – we give thanks to God for His many gifts and graces to us. We thank Him with special fervour this evening for the ministry and the witness which Fr Neal Carlin and his brothers and sisters in Christ in the Columba Community have given in this diocese of Derry and beyond it, both individually and collectively, up to the present time. We thank God for who they are and for what they do. Secondly, we invoke the guidance, the courage and the strength of the Holy Spirit on their ongoing ministry and witness in the future.

Gratitude

Bishops must exercise discernment in deciding which movement or initiative or apostolate they can endorse and approve. For many years I have been aware of the work of the Columba Community. Since coming here as Bishop of Derry, I made it my business to inquire and research further the scope, nature and quality of the Community's work. At the end of all of that, and with the willing and enthusiastic assent of my advisors, I now immediately avail of this opportunity to thank Fr Neal Carlin and all the members of the Columba Community for their work, their ministry and their personal witness. In formally expressing my thanks, which I do in the name of the Diocese of Derry, I am simply articulating a gratitude which has been tacitly but sincerely felt for many years.

Approval

In expressing my gratitude I wish also to give more tangible expression to that gratitude by stating that from now onwards I approve of the ministry of healing, of reconciliation and of prayer of the Columba Community. I commend it to the people for their participation in it and I commend it to God in the sure and certain hope that all who 'till and plant and water' under the guidance of the Holy Spirit, as the Columba Community does, will reap a bountiful harvest which is in the gift of the Lord and Master of the vineyard alone to give.

Role of the Bishop

The Columba Community will continue to exercise its apostolate in Columba House in Queen Street, Derry, and in St Anthony's Retreat Centre, Dundrean, Co. Donegal. Canonically, it is a private association of the faithful with its own constitution, which has been accepted and approved by me. The Community has developed its own ethos and enjoys its own autonomy; both of these elements will be respected. The canonical recognition which I am now according the Columba Community very clearly and explicitly entails that for the future the Local Ordinary not only may but must exercise a supervisory role. This will result in a constructive and in an active relationship between the diocese and the Community which, I have every confidence, will be mutually advantageous. The more precise and formal details of this relationship, which are governed by Canon Law, have been duly agreed, noted and recorded elsewhere.

Ecumenical dimension

I have been aware of the ecumenical awareness of the Columba Community and of its work in promoting Christian Unity. I note that this awareness is given practical and welcome expression tonight by the presence among us of the Revd Cecil Kerr, with whom Fr Neal has worked so closely. I welcome you to the Cathedral this evening and I thank you for coming. I commend the pursuit of Christian Unity to the prayers and activities of the Columba Community. In doing so, I remind the Community that the unity for which Jesus prayed will only be achieved by prayer and by living out faithfully, in honesty and in truth one's own inherited faith tradition and faith expression. The closer we come to Christ the closer we come to one another. Cosmetic compromises misrepresent authentic ecumenism and make the ideal for which Jesus prayed more difficult to achieve.

Ministry of healing and reconciliation

Of all the activities in which the Columba Community is engaged, prayer has the first place and appropriately so. The centrality of the Eucharist is very much the 'source and summit' of the spirituality of the Community. From prayer and the Eucharist the Community is led and inspired to express the faith which is in them in a practical outreach of an apostolic and a Christian kind, to their brothers and sisters in the wider community. Perhaps the work for which the Community is best known and respected is their ministry of healing and reconciliation. This has been a valued, an important and a much availed of service over many years, when many people then as now stood in need of healing and of being reconciled with others and with God. I thank God for gifting Fr Carlin with a special charism in this regard. May that gift grow further, flourish and yield an abundant harvest.

The ministry of healing and reconciliation must be a priority for all of us at this time. Today there is more rather than less need for the ministry of healing and reconciliation among so many of God's people who stand in need of healing of all kinds, and who need to be reconciled with one another and with God. Bringing people to that awareness, calling them, and facilitating them to be healed and reconciled as individuals, as groups, as communities puts those who are active in this very sensitive and specialised area of pastoral work in the front line of peacemakers and peace-builders. True peace will only be achieved when social, personal, psychological, moral scars are healed and when reconciliation replaces suspicion with trust, acrimony with respect, ignorance with understanding, hatred with love. This is just a part of the challenge which faces all of us at this time. This healing and reconciliation process must not be seen as the preserve or the responsibility of the few – it must be shared by all – but it is reassuring to know that there is a resource available to us which has a tried, tested and proven record in this regard. We can all make the prayer of St Francis our own at this time, 'Lord, make me an instrument of your peace ...'. For that, Lord, we pray, especially today the first anniversary of the Republican ceasefire.

The future faced with hope

It remains to be seen how, under the guidance of the Holy Spirit, the Columba Community will evolve and develop in the future. Provided they keep the focus and the emphasis which they have now on prayer, on reading and meditating on God's word, on discerning in the Spirit, on invoking the patronage and protection of Mary, and most importantly as long as they remain so strongly Eucharistic, I am confident that the Lord, at the appropriate time, will indicate the way in which the Community should go. It is interesting to note the growing interest among people of all ages who feel called to live their faith and give witness in a particularly compelling way by living in community, by a life of intense prayer and apostolic commitment by the taking of simple, solemn vows. This, as you know, has been a feature of the monastic tradition in the Church for many centuries and it appears to be emerging with renewed vigour in more recent times. That is not the direction in which the Columba Community is now going and it may not be the way it will decide to go in the future. I hope that the Community will be open and receptive to assist and facilitate those men and women in the future who might feel called to live their baptismal commitment in this specialised way, and who may be seeking a facility such as the Columba Community offers to test what they perceive to be their special vocation. In this way, and in so many others, I look forward to the Columba Community being at the service of the local church. Precisely, in this context, I note the interest of the Columba Community in Celtic spirituality and in Celtic monasticism. It might be helpful, it certainly would be interesting, to explore this aspect further by researching the principles of Celtic spirituality and to assess their relevance and their application in our own day.

Travelling together on the journey
This is a very happy occasion. In one sense, the Columba Community has arrived. In another much more accurate sense, I would suggest, it is just beginning its journey, or rather another stage in the journey which began some years ago. Our prayers and good wishes are with Fr Neal and with all within the Community and outside of it who journey with them. In Peru a

word very dear to the Peruvians is *accompanar*, to accompany, to be fellow travellers with, to support, to show interest, to care. Let us all *accompanar* the Columba Community on their journey. I know that they will welcome our companionship and honour our trust. May the Lord who has begun this good work in you bring it to a fruitful conclusion for his own greater honour and glory. Peace be with you.

Most Revd Séamus Hegarty
Bishop of Derry

Complementary Models of the Church

The priest and collaborative ministry in parish and in small Christian communities

When I first began to think about the future of the Church in Ireland, I considered writing a separate chapter on the priesthood of the future, as distinct from a chapter on the model of the Church to come. However, on reflection, it would seem that one chapter of this book on the future Church, including the role of the priest, would convey what I have in mind. This puts the priest in his proper position in relation to the vocation of all Christians in building the Kingdom of God on earth.

The primary work of a priest is to offer sacrifice. This may seem to be a very traditional definition of his role but, the fact is, that is why he is ordained. So let us tease out what that means in terms of his preaching and living the Gospel.

When we priests say 'this is my body' and 'this is my blood', we are called to be an *alter Christus*, as we were told long ago in the seminary. Followers of Christ are *all* called to be that, yet the priest, in particular, is to lead the way. He is to allow Christ to rule and be alive within. He is called to serve as Christ did and encourage all baptised people to release Christ from the temple within, and to serve the poor and spiritually starving of the world.

This is what the priest has been educated to do and set aside to do. He has no family or material issues to worry him. It is in this regard that his celibacy and single life have meaning. He is free to pray more. In not being called to give focused attention to one family, he is free to give his life to all. So when, in obedience to Christ, he says, 'This is My Body, this is My Blood', he is certainly recalling the reality of the everlasting sacrifice of Christ, yet he is also uniting in Christ's spirit of love and generosity.

Here, he is invited to offer his own life as bread to feed others; to offer his energy, time, attention and, indeed, his life's blood, for the good people around God's altar and around God's world. It is this attitude of being ready to be broken, and even crucified for preaching the true radical gospel, that is central to Christ's sacrificial priesthood.

It is in this spirit that we pray and work for the building up of God's kingdom. At the risk of getting into profound theology, I quote Pope Benedict XVI on this point:

> As an *alter Christus*, the priest is profoundly united to the Word of the Father who, in becoming incarnate took the form of a servant, he became a servant (Phil 2:5–11). The priest is a servant of Christ, in the sense that his existence, configured to Christ ontologically, acquires an essentially relational character: he is in Christ, for Christ and with Christ, at the service of humankind. Because he belongs to Christ, the priest is radically at the service of all people: he is the minister of their salvation, their happiness and their authentic liberation, developing, in this gradual assumption of Christ's will, in prayer, in 'being heart to heart' with him. Therefore this is the indispensable condition for every proclamation, which entails participation in the sacramental offering of the Eucharist and docile obedience to the Church.
>
> *Pope Benedict XVI, 24 June 2009*

The preaching on the power of the Cross and the self-giving it calls for will, indeed, offend a worldly mind formed outside the believing community. Sadly, it may even give offence and be a scandal to a certain type of Church member. This type of member will generally be materially well-off, have ambition for power and position, and be fearful of any radical Christian who attempts to empower the weak, the poor and the marginalised. This type can only be converted by the love and forgiveness of the Lord, just as Paul was converted on the way to Damascus.

In this regard, I often think of the wisdom of God in leading Paul to the house of Ananias for his full recovery. The legalistic, self-righteous Paul is healed of blindness by the defenceless Ananias whom he came to imprison, or perhaps put to death. Only Jesus can, by His cross, bridge the gap between the two, the persecutor and the persecuted; the legalistic, ego-centric, religious defender Saul and the spiritually awakened Ananias, who was set free by Jesus' sacrifice and not by the Law.

If we priests, few as we are in number these days, are to give of our best for a new type of Church to spring up, I would suggest that new opportunities abound. Although, at first glance these may look more like challenges than opportunities.

Radical changes have taken place in values over the past twenty years or so. Whether it has been in the area of substance abuse, violence leading to almost weekly murders, availability of pornography and the level of sexual promiscuity, undoubtedly our Irish society seems to have lost its moral compass. Some call it moral free fall.

Many parents will tell you they do not have control of their teenage children and they blame the fact that 'society has changed'. They speak as if they are victims of an external peer group pressure over which they have no control. Perhaps that is true to some extent, but it could also be an excuse in forfeiting responsibility for the safeguarding of their children. The times we live in certainly offer a challenge and an opportunity to priests and Christian leaders; I cannot see other elements, or statutory bodies, facing the moral decline we speak about here and doing anything about it.

The media have certainly added to the problem by under-mining family values and condemning our entire Church ways because of the terrible sins of the few. We cannot, it seems, look to Government for the spiritual or moral revival society requires.

The vulnerable, the outsider and the hungry
in today's society needing the Christian message
I live at St Anthony's Retreat Centre, on a plateau in the Donegal countryside. As I write this, I am looking out at sheep huddled together in mid-winter, knee-deep in mud near the gate of a barren, wet field. They await being fed by the farmer, who will eventually arrive with hay and nuts. They seem so powerless and defenceless against the hail and the wind. They seem so dependent. They would starve to death if it were not for the shepherd, the farmer. To me, they are an image of our Catholic people in Ireland, who were conditioned to be overly dependent on the priest for their spiritual nourishment and moral values.

If we look at the mission of Jesus, He is always empowering the marginalised and the poor, the prostitutes, lame, the sick, or alienated gentile, the widow and the children. Jesus is persecuted, as indeed prophets still often are, by the power-hungry religious and the political figures who seek control.

The question for the clergy and laity who seek renewal in Christ today in Ireland is surely this: how do we find ways of following Christ and building his kingdom among his people, especially among the marginalised and isolated, the fear-filled aged, the unemployed, the angry, redundant, and tomorrow's potential emigrants, the disillusioned youth?

These are the sick, hungry flock that have not yet experienced the Word made flesh living among them and comforting them. How can they experience being listened to and respected even if they have wandered away from the flock at times in search of green pastures; even when they have got entangled amid the briars or, for a while, amid the ravines and crevices where they may have been frightened?

The youth, in particular, whom we have been coming to get treatment for drugs, alcohol and gambling addictions, show a common trait: they often are twenty-five or thirty, going on sixteen or seventeen years of age. Somehow, because of the escape into drugs and alcohol as young teenagers, their growth emotionally and spiritually has been stunted. Psychologically, they seem to me to have gone into a backwash in the river of life. They have, like pieces of debris we see swirling around in a whirlpool at the side of a river, simply not moved on through the challenging but necessary growing pains of adolescence. Getting them to grow up and be more responsible for their lives, and choices, is the task of a good treatment centre.

Male spirituality weekends, where the young man is encouraged through a type of initiation into manhood, can also be very helpful. In a society where teens have a healthy relationship with elders, and especially parents and grandparents who are good role models, these programmes are unnecessary. But today, like in no age we know of previously, teens have little or no communication with grandparents, largely due to television and computer games.

The wisdom of the ages and especially the values that faith brings, in the past, were transmitted by grandparents to children. The stories told around the family hearth, or kitchen table, were part of a valuable legacy, but the human relationships were even more important in fostering a healthy adolescent.

The good news from places like White Oaks Rehabilitation Centre is that when people come in from the cold, even for a month's treatment, a month's respite for the family, often betterment takes place. This is especially true when the client has hit rock bottom. Then they often find better health, inner peace and a way forward.

Possible new communities – within the parish setting
If the White Oaks Rehabilitation Centre for us, in the Columba Community, has been both a challenge and an inspiration, surely similar social economic problems can be addressed by good, relevant pastoral councils looking at some of the categories mentioned above. Such a pastoral council, or basic Christian community group, needs to acknowledge that the Lord's Spirit is paramount.

We need to ask the Lord as we pray together and as individuals if we are the people to respond to this particular work, at this particular time, in this particular area. This would be to employ the Catholic Worker Method. This method proved very fruitful to us when we met to pray back in 1979, and looked at what God was saying to the Church and to us in the signs of the times in which we lived.

The method is summed up in the three words – See, Judge and Act. It did not take a lot of listening prayer back then to figure out that a gospel of peace and reconciliation was relevant, not only for prisoners and families, but for society in general in this land.

It is vital that the Lord who is in charge of his people and his church is listened to as 'unless the Lord builds the house, in vain do the labourers build it'. We should have learned by now that good ideas, or apparently good programmes, simply will not cut it. We need to be guided by God's idea. Let us not think that is a pious thing.

As we see in Jeremiah 31 and quoted in Hebrews 8:10, 'I will place my Laws in their minds and I will write them upon their hearts.' In other words, Jeremiah is foretelling the Christian era when the Holy Spirit, by His guidance, leads His people into truth. That is what guided the Early Church and any powerful reform throughout the ages. This is how St Francis was led when the Spirit said to him 'rebuild my Church'.

The priest and suicide awareness

A few days prior to writing this I was approached by a young priest. I was impressed by his zeal for the befriending of relatives of those who had died by suicide. He told me that he had been the only cleric present at a large gathering of the bereaved due to suicide.

I was aware that such a group existed in the Derry area. Some of them once visited us here on a residential weekend. When I asked their leader how come no clergy from any denomination was involved, she replied, 'Many of these people have had a bad experience of Church.'

At one time, in my experience, the parish priest was involved in too many things. Nowadays, he is in danger of becoming irrelevant, or uninvolved in the things that matter to people's lives. So, I encouraged this young priest to stay with the group. One day, I trust he will build a basic Christian community around this vulnerable group, just as we have developed a Christian ministry with the alcoholics and some ex-prisoners. His role will be to live out the sacrificial priesthood in that group. He will, as described earlier, fulfil his vocation in praying for, and with that group, so that one day, as St Peter's letter says, they will receive a Christian spiritual awakening themselves. He needs to persevere in being a lamp and an example to them 'until the day breaks through and the Morning Star arises in your hearts.' (2 Peter 1:19)

There could be similar Christian communities for the categories of people I mentioned earlier. There will always be need for the traditional pastoral ministries within a given parish, such as caring for the sick, visiting the homes of the parishioners and supporting the teachers and parents in their role as educators, as well as administering the sacraments, and being a blessing and consolation to the bereaved.

However, I sense we will see some clergy drawn to a ministry involving the social and economic needs of God's people. These dimensions of people's lives ought never to be deliberated upon in isolation. We need to look at them in the light of our faith and trust in a God who cares for all our needs. The priest, for example, is ideally placed to gather together a think-tank of people locally to look at the plight of the unemployed.

Again, we look for our example of this to the basic Christian community movement in the developing world, especially in Central Africa and South America. There, the local need, be it for clean water, proper roads, better housing or sewerage system, is looked at by the praying community, who study the Bible and examine what the Word of God has to say to them. Here, they believe, they will find a way forward. They act together.

This is the kind of spirituality and faith that moves mountains, develops collaborative ministry and binds people together in Christian fellowship. Unless we, as clergy, get involved in this type of social gospel and can bring Christ's Gospel to the marketplace, we will have lost this age to materialism or despair.

As Pope Francis said, the people of God want pastors, not clergy acting like bureaucrats or government officials. If we are to walk the pathway of the flock in our care, we will, indeed, get our boots dirty. Then again, this Pope argues that is the way to go. This sounds so grounded and earthy that it appeals to me, but too many of us, especially in recent times, have not been ready to walk that path.

I, like many others, need to be led by the good shepherd along such ways and not await eternally further utterances from Pope Francis, inspiring as they may be. As one wise priest friend, J.J. O'Riordan told me a few years ago: 'When we find ourselves preoccupied and talking more about bishops, Church structures and, indeed, the Pope, than we are talking about Jesus Christ, then we can be sure that we are out of sync as a local Church.'

I return, again, to our own example locally. In 2000, there was simply a green field in a poor border area, here in Donegal. Now, we employ some thirty-four people in total, between the Organic Acorn Initiative, the Celtic Peace Garden initiative and the White Oaks Rehabilitation Centre. We never set out to be big employers, but these things have their own momentum when they are begun in the right spirit.

More importantly, this place offers men and women the dignity that work, affirmation and good environment gives. If growing organic vegetables in an economically poor area of Donegal is possible, surely similar ventures could be part of building up the Kingdom of God and a holistic Church in other areas throughout Ireland.

The Stained Vessel

The glass was always to be clean and,
being transparent,
would allow the clear Light and Sacred Presence within
to shine forth for all the world.
The bearers of Christ were, and are,
called to be a light on the hilltop,
and be a light to the people who walked in darkness.
We were called to be a sign of hope in a despairing society.
Did not Jesus say, 'Let your light shine so brightly before men
that seeing your good works
they would glorify your Father in Heaven'?
When the glass container has been so deeply stained,
so engrained with stain and grime that it instead blots
and blocks out the beauty of its contents
from man's vision,
what then?
Surely, it requires to be scalded, deeply purged
and treated with the appropriate detergent
of penance and fasting,
so that it might shine again with God's mercy.
Even if it is to be reshaped and reformed in the refiners fire,
let His will be done.
It is, indeed, time for meltdown;
time to hand the vineyard back to the Lord.
It is time now to seriously seek the Lord's will for us,

His Church, the people of God.
This is the Kairos time,
a time in which we are called to be reshaped and reformed.
Like the addict, who accepts his/her powerlessness
and then turns to the Higher Power,
we are all called to experience
The Lordship of Jesus Christ over His Church.

Time to Rejoice

Lord, refresh my heart.
Scatter the residual pain
that crowds my mind and
leaves my senses sluggish.
Refresh my soul
with bursting spring water
from Your risen Easter presence.
Let me be alive
and not sleep in agony in the garden,
or be dead on the cross any longer.
Amen.
For it is time to sing. Alleluia.
For it is time to rejoice.
Amen.

The Victory Dance of the Son of David

With the lined cloths used to wrap your Crucified Body,
You, Lord, made a banner to swing and flow
around your Bright Brow.
The Angels join you now,
as they did the night you were born.
Mary, your mother, then marvelled
at the words spoken about you.
She later wept
when sword pierced heart,
but now with You rejoices.
All is, was, will be, well.
In You and with You
we celebrate.
Your Sacred Wound has won us over.
All is well.
All is well. We have tasted Love
and, should we never do another thing, it's all ok.
All is well.
Should we never write another psalm of praise
or sing another song,
all is well.
I hand over to you fully
when I have nothing else to do to prove
I love you.
I hand over to you

when I have nothing else to experience here to prove
your love for me.
So, then, we are at Peace.
So, then, enjoy the Truth.
Be at Peace.

Conclusion

I trust the reader has enjoyed the various components of this book. I certainly have enjoyed writing it and recalling the journey so far.

This book has been about waiting upon, or trusting the Lord. It is about listening prayer and a readiness to act courageously in obedience to the Lord's will.

The concept of obedience, like the word 'power', has had a bad track record, due to misuse and abuse. The word obedience derives from the Latin word *ob* meaning towards and *audire* meaning hearing. Towards hearing surely includes listening. Jesus' obedience to the Father and His good use of power need to be looked at and imitated. We need to allow him to redeem these concepts so that we, his co-heirs of the Father, can enjoy true obedience and proper use of power in the service of people. Jesus 'only did what he saw the Father doing' and said 'only what the Father gave him to say'.

The building of Columba House of Prayer and Reconciliation in Derry was the fruit of listening to the Holy Spirit, as was St Anthony's Retreat Centre and the other facilities on the Donegal border area. For 'unless the Lord builds the house, they labour in vain who build it'.

While on the one hand this book is an autobiography, the story centres on the formation and work of the Columba Community of Prayer and Reconciliation over the past thirty-five years. This, I regard, as a prophetic model for the Church of the future.

I wish to express my gratitude for all who have accompanied us on the journey. It was a different journey, no doubt, and often misunderstood and sometimes opposed. However, it was a noble journey and was always blessed.

The Lord forgave our mistakes and frailty, and did not allow them to spoil His plan. Over the years we waited, we prayed, we built. We also struggled, wept and, indeed, laughed.

'We were left to feel like men condemned to death so that we might trust, not on ourselves, but in God who raises the dead. He rescued us from the danger of death and will continue to do so. We have put our hope in Him who will never cease to deliver us. But you must help us with your prayers, so that on our behalf God may be thanked for the gift granted us through the prayers of so many' (2 Corinthians 1:10–11).

May the reader enjoy his/her own journey. Remember, life is what takes place as we wait for something else to happen. May that something else for you be the fullness that is stored up for us in Heaven.

Slán libh,
Neal Carlin